Six Billion and Counting

Six Billion and Counting

Population Growth and Food Security in the 21st Century

Klaus M. Leisinger
Karin Schmitt
Rajul Pandya-Lorch

Published by the International Food Policy Research Institute
Washington, D.C.

Distributed by The Johns Hopkins University Press

Library of Congress Cataloging-in-Publication Data

Leisinger, Klaus M.
  Six billion and counting : population growth and food security in the 21st century/
Klaus M. Leisinger, Karin Schmitt, and Rajul Pandya-Lorch.
    p. cm.
  Includes bibliographical references and index.
  ISBN 0-89629-705-5 (paper)
    1. Population forecasting. 2. Overpopulation. 3. Population—Environmental aspects. 4.
Food supply. I. Schmitt, Karin. II. Pandya-Lorch, Rajul. III. Title.

HB849.53 .L44 2001
363.8—dc21   2001039391

Contents

Foreword   vii
Per Pinstrup-Andersen

Preface   ix
Klaus M. Leisinger, Karin M. Schmitt, Rajul Pandya-Lorch

Acknowledgments   xiii

Chapter 1   **Six Billion and Counting**   1

Chapter 2   **From Population Theory to Reality**   19

Chapter 3   **Social and Economic Impacts of Rapid Population Growth**   31

Chapter 4   **Pressures on Natural Systems**   41

Chapter 5   **Assuring Food Security for a Growing Population**   57

Chapter 6   **Population and Sociocultural Norms in Traditional Societies**   77

Chapter 7   **Prerequisites for Responsible Population Policies**   97

Chapter 8   **The Battle for a Better Future**   113

Notes   129

Index   149

About the Authors   155

Foreword

The International Food Policy Research Institute has long worked to clarify the kinds of policies that can help developing countries achieve sustainable food security for their people. The difficulty of achieving this task, however, can be greatly eased or exacerbated depending on the number of people a country must feed. Rapid population growth can make the burden of ensuring food security much greater than it would otherwise be.

In *Six Billion and Counting*, Klaus Leisinger, Karin Schmitt, and Rajul Pandya-Lorch take a careful look at why populations grow so rapidly in some areas and at the consequences of this growth. In many cases, causes and consequences are related. Social and economic conditions, for example, both inform and are informed by rates of population growth. Economic hardship can cause parents to have more children to serve as "social security" in their old age, but parents with more children invest less in the education and health of each child and may thus make it harder for these children to climb out of poverty.

Some people argue that human ingenuity has heretofore found ways of pushing back the limits on the Earth's carrying capacity and will continue to do so. Can new technologies such as agricultural biotechnology and techniques for efficient energy use ensure a sustainable, healthy life for all the world's people, even under conditions of rapid population growth? Not indefinitely, say Leisinger and his co-authors. What these technologies can do, however, is to buy the world time to put policies in place for reducing population growth.

Such policies, the authors explain, must be humane, seeking not just to reduce population growth but to improve the quality of human life. Policies must address the complex and interrelated causes of population growth, focusing on women's roles and opportunities, urbanization and migration, education and health care, social security systems, and environmental degradation, for instance. And any attempt to achieve sustainable development and food security must deal with the high share of resources consumed in the world's industrial countries.

Finally, *Six Billion and Counting* makes the point that the world's failure to achieve greater progress in reducing population growth arises not because we cannot do it, but because we are too complacent to do it. The policies that are most likely to work are well known, but the political will to implement them is lacking. International agreements on population have not so far generated this political will. Let us hope it will not take a humanitarian crisis for the world's leaders to find a reason to act.

Per Pinstrup-Andersen
Director General
International Food Policy Research Institute

Preface

Today is a very special day: never before have so many people inhabited Earth. Yet whenever you read these words, yesterday was special for the same reason. Moreover, the same will be true tomorrow, and the day after that, and every succeeding day for at least the next 50 years. Since you started reading this paragraph, world population has increased by more than 50 people.

World population has more than doubled since the end of World War II. Despite substantial advances and countless activities in the areas of family health and family planning over the past 30 years, global population has continued to grow by about 80 million people each year. This means that Earth has more than 150 new inhabitants every minute. Global population reached 6 billion in the second half of 1999, and will rise to at least 9 billion in the next 50 years.

Dramatic changes in food production, processing, and trade in recent decades have provided enough food, if equally distributed, to meet the basic needs of every person on Earth. A doubling of the grain harvest and tripling of livestock production since the early sixties have made about 2,800 calories available per person per day. Yet more than 800 million people—almost one eighth of humanity—are "food-insecure." In other words, they cannot produce or purchase enough food at all times to lead healthy, productive lives. Astonishing advances in agricultural productivity and human ingenuity during the twentieth century did not translate into a world free of hunger and malnutrition.

These are the facts. But what is the meaning of such facts? When we began work on this book, we were determined not to dramatize the effects of global population growth. Six years ago, two of us wrote a book on this topic, and we assumed that updating population statistics, while also revising the text, would be sufficient to take account of developments in the intervening years. But this proved to be impossible. Too much had changed—some things for the better, but much for the worse, particularly with respect to the availability of water and arable land, and destruction of tropical forests. The fact that the world's population had increased by about 600 million during those six years also put greater stress on food supplies and social carrying capacity.

We were struck—and alarmed—by the social, ecological, economic, and political consequences of population growth. Many countries already have a difficult time avoiding conflicts over allocation of resources at their current population levels. If their populations continue to grow, conflicts over available resources are inevitable. Wherever these conflicts occur, social order is undermined. This social disorder in turn leads to an increase in poverty. Once this happens, the conditions needed to reduce birth rates are no longer present.

Sub-Saharan Africa is particularly threatened by these developments. It is the only region in the world where poverty, hunger, and child malnutrition have increased and the quality of life has declined. According to the United Nations Development Programme, half of the people in sub-Saharan Africa were living in absolute poverty by 2000. The spread of AIDS, which has reached epidemic proportions in this region, is canceling out gains made in reducing infant mortality and increasing life expectancy. Virtually nowhere else in the world are disparities so great and the quality of government so poor. In Nigeria, where petroleum exports have brought in more than $200 billion in the last decade, per capita income remains as low as it was 30 years ago. Almost 120 million women in sub-Saharan Africa are illiterate. Moreover, African women now have less access to education and land than ever before. It is difficult to make progress in curtailing population growth under such conditions.

The aim of this book is to look at the consequences of continued population growth for our resource systems and for national and global food security. It will proceed as soberly as possible, despite the reasons for alarm. Book sales might well be increased and the authors' reputations enhanced if every identifiable negative trend were extrapolated, and if only arguments for worst-case scenarios were presented, culminating in a dramatic prophesy of the end of the world soon in the new millennium. But this would not do justice to the complexity of the situation, nor would it allow for sufficiently serious analysis of a diverse set of problems.

This book does not pretend to base its conclusions about population policy on science alone. As in all things political, any assessment of the circumstances related to population policy depends to a great extent on personal value judgments and individual definitions of issues. "Neutrality" in the social sciences has never existed, nor will it. Values are, by definition, the very standards by which we judge importance.

Solving the population problem can be viewed as determining at the outset what ultimate values should be pursued. Some values related to population policy are widely held. Reducing illiteracy is a common goal because it is generally thought valuable for human beings to possess the means of achieving knowledge. The elimination of hunger and malnutrition is sought because of the self-evident fact that human beings must eat to survive. The preservation of nonrenewable resources is necessary in order for human life to continue through future generations. There is little argument about the validity of these propositions, because they all presuppose some important human values: knowledge, life, and survival of the species.

Yet many basic values appear to come into conflict in population issues: the well-being of future generations versus that of the present generation, the public welfare versus the individual's freedom to procreate, and so on. When such basic values clash, we confront the most fundamental ethical choices. This book, therefore, goes beyond scientific assessments of the population issue to consider these choices in detail.

Klaus M. Leisinger
Karin M. Schmitt
Rajul Pandya-Lorch
Washington, D.C.
January 2002

Acknowledgments

We wish to thank Linda Starke for her more than valuable assistance in editing the manuscript. Her skill in melding the writings of three authors with three different styles into a coherent whole is simply exceptional.

For dedicated support in helping to make this volume possible, we also wish to thank Heidi Fritschel, senior editor at the International Food Policy Research Institute (IFPRI), who assisted inexhaustibly in editing the manuscript, compiling the notes, and otherwise keeping the project on track.

In addition, we were greatly assisted by Carl Haub, senior demographer at the Population Reference Bureau, who provided us with the most recent population figures, thus helping make the information in this book as accurate and relevant as possible.

Finally, we are grateful to Klaus von Grebmer at IFPRI for recognizing the importance of the topic, for encouraging us to publish with the Institute, and for devoting personal time to the preparation and the publishing of this volume.

Chapter 1

Six Billion and Counting

The following words spoken by a politician may sound familiar:

> One thing is sure: the Earth is more cultivated and developed now than ever before; there is more farming but fewer forests, swamps are drying up and cities springing up on an unprecedented scale. We have become a burden to our planet. Resources are becoming scarce and soon Nature will no longer be able to satisfy our needs. It will come to pass that disease, hunger, flood and war will reduce the excessively large numbers of the human species.[1]

This statement dates from the year 200 BC and was made by the Roman politician Quintus Septimus Tertullianus. Fortunately, Tertullianus has been proved wrong so far.

Yet never before in human history has the population of Earth been as great as it is today, and never before in the history of civilization has it grown so rapidly within one century (see Table 1). People born before 1960 are the first generation in history who will witness a doubling of the world's population in their lifetimes, while those born in or before 1927 have seen a tripling.

The fertility rate—the number of births in a woman's lifetime—has declined steadily since the sixties, owing to social and cultural changes but also to a massive increase in efforts to provide acceptable methods of family planning. Yet annual world population growth continued to increase in absolute terms until the second half of the eighties.

The average (median) age in the world—27 years—is young. In sub-Saharan Africa, 45 percent of the population is under the age of 15. In other words, almost half of the population in this region has not even reached childbearing age. Data for

Table 1   World Population Growth by Billions

World population in billions	Year	Time needed to reach this level
One	1804	All of human history
Two	1927	123 years
Three	1960	33 years
Four	1974	14 years
Five	1987	13 years
Six	1999	12 years
Seven[a]	2012	13 years
Eight[a]	2026	14 years
Nine[a]	2043	17 years

Source: United Nations Population Division, *World Population Prospects: The 2000 Revision*, Vol. 1 (New York: 2001).
[a]Projected population growth (medium variant).

developing countries on other continents are equally alarming: in Asia, 35 percent of the population is under the age of 15, and in Latin America, 33 percent.

Even on the utopian assumption that birth rates in all developing countries will decline immediately to the level at which parents merely "replace" themselves, which is just above two children, absolute population growth will still remain high for many years. The dynamics already set in motion by a youthful age structure ensure that population will double in most of these countries.

There must come a point when population growth threatens global food security and the Earth's finite natural resources. More people mean greater demand for food, water, education, health care, sanitary infrastructure, and jobs, as well as greater pressure on the environment.

What specific threats does population growth present now and in the coming decades? How can the world achieve sustainable development in the face of an ever-growing population? To what degree can this task be accomplished through human inventiveness and new technology? How important is it to drastically slow population growth? What are the elements of an effective and human-centered population policy? These are the questions this book seeks to answer.

Current and Projected Population Growth

Never before in human history has the world experienced such a pronounced demographic success as in the past 30 years. Birth rates decreased faster, over a longer period of time, in more countries, and to lower levels than ever before.

At an annual rate of 1.2 percent, world population is growing more slowly today than at its historic high point in the late sixties, when the rate was 2.04 percent (see Figure 1). Annual growth in absolute terms, currently at 77 million, is also

Figure 1 Population Growth Rates for the World and Major Regions, 1950–2050

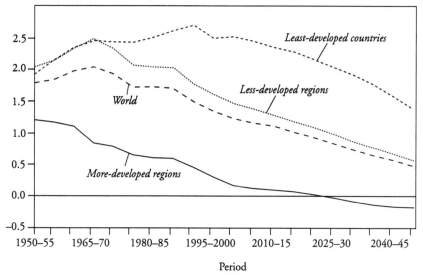

Source: United Nations Population Division, *World Population Prospects: The 2000 Revision* (New York, 2001).

beneath its historic high point of almost 86 million in the eighties. Some 97 percent of this growth still takes place in developing countries. Indeed, according to the United Nations, half of world population growth occurs in just six countries: India, China, Pakistan, Nigeria, Bangladesh, and Indonesia.

In absolute terms, Asia contributes the most to world population growth, at 50 million people a year, while Africa accounts for only 17 million, although at 2.36 percent, Africa's rate of growth is the highest. Two of every five people alive today are living in China or India. While 10 nations currently have populations that exceed 100 million, this number is expected to rise to 19 by 2050. The variance in rates of population growth among individual countries will be responsible for substantial change in the top 10 contributors to world population growth in this century (see Table 2).

As great as growth has been in the past 50 years, world population is still expected to grow by at least 3 billion and perhaps by almost 5 billion in the next 50 years, depending on which fertility variant among U.N. projections proves true (see Figure 2).[2] Discussions in this book are based exclusively on the medium-fertility projection. This projection may turn out to be optimistic, however, if too little is

Table 2   Ten Largest Countries in 2000, with Projection of Ten Largest in 2050

Position	Country	Population in 2000 (million)	Country	Population in 2050* (million)
1	China	1,275	India	1,572
2	India	1,009	China	1,462
3	United States	283	United States	397
4	Indonesia	212	Pakistan	344
5	Brazil	170	Indonesia	311
6	Russia	145	Nigeria	279
7	Pakistan	141	Bangladesh	265
8	Bangladesh	137	Brazil	247
9	Japan	127	D.R. Congo	204
10	Nigeria	114	Ethiopia	186

* Medium-fertility variant projections.

Source: United Nations Population Division, *World Population Prospects: The 2000 Revision*, Vol. 1 (New York: 2001).

done to implement the Programme of Action adopted in 1994 at the International Conference on Population and Development in Cairo. Delegates to this meeting reached a general consensus about the role of population growth in the development process and agreed about what constitutes humane population policy and what strategies are appropriate for pursuing it.[3] The international community pledged to commit $17 billion by 2000 to implement the main points agreed upon at the conference—a tripling of resources within five years. Industrial countries agreed to provide one third of the necessary resources by 2000. This pledge has not been honored.

Success Stories

Past experience shows that we are capable of planning and implementing actions that can improve the lives of millions. The world has made important progress in slowing population growth, improving the food security and quality of life of the world's people, and protecting the natural resources on which development depends. In fact, developing countries have made more social, economic, ecological, and political progress in the last 30 years than today's industrial countries did in more than a century.

Social Progress

The leading social indicators over the last 30–40 years reveal one of the most spectacular success stories in the history of civilization: people alive today lead longer lives than human beings ever have before.

- Average life expectancy at birth has risen by more than one third in developing countries. Today it exceeds 62 years in at least 120 countries with a total popu-

Figure 2   World Population, 1950–2050

Population (billions)

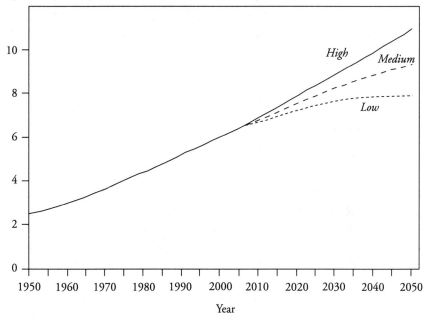

Source: See Figure 1.

lation of over 5 billion people. In 1955, the global average was only 48; today it is 66, and is expected to reach 73 by 2025.[4]

• The child mortality rate in developing countries has declined by more than half since the sixties, from 149 per 1,000 live births to 62 as of 1999.

• The share of the population with access to clean water in developing countries has more than doubled and now exceeds 70 percent.

• Total enrollment in primary schools has risen by more than two thirds, and the adult illiteracy rate has dropped by almost half.

• Important progress has been made in controlling contagious diseases: the number of people suffering from leprosy has been reduced by four fifths, and smallpox has been eradicated.

Food Security Progress

Never before in human history has more food, arguably of greater variety and better and safer quality, been produced. Although many people are still hungry and malnourished in this world of plenty, progress is being made in tackling food insecurity.

- The global production of cereals has increased by 133 percent since 1961, production of meat rose by 233 percent, and the output of roots and tubers increased by 50 percent. Despite population growth during this period, per capita food availability has increased by 24 percent to almost 2,800 calories per day.

- Production increases were driven by improvements in productivity; for instance, cereal yields worldwide rose from 1.4 tons per hectare in the early sixties to 3 tons in the late nineties. Yet while yields increased rapidly—in China, for example, from 1.2 tons to 4.7 tons during this period—they remained stagnant at around 1 ton in sub-Saharan Africa.

- The proportion of the world that is food-insecure or chronically malnourished was cut in half—from 37 percent in 1969/71 to 18 percent in 1995/97.

- The share of preschool children who are malnourished or severely underweight for their age dropped from 47 percent in 1970 to 31 percent in 1995.

Economic Progress

Enormous economic progress has been made as well, especially since the eighties, although it has not taken place consistently throughout the world. In general, however, greater gains have been made in the fight against poverty in the last 50 years than in the preceding 500. Even the recent financial crises in Asia and Latin America have done little to change this picture. For the first time in history, the eradication of poverty is in sight—provided that the necessary political commitment can be mobilized. Specific efforts to implement economic reforms have also helped many of the world's poorest countries to make significant economic progress.

Ecological Progress

The greatest ecological advances in the last 30 years have taken place at the institutional level, in the form of international cooperation and through collaboration with the private sector.[5] Awareness of ecological issues has risen in every industrial country, and environmental issues have now become a powerful political factor. As a result industrial countries have devised and applied more ecologically sound laws, economic instruments, technologies, and production processes. Most industrial countries have significantly reduced the problems of water and air pollution. Moreover, other local environmental indicators (noise emissions, heavy metal contamination) have shown similar improvement.

New and ecologically efficient technologies and practices are now available for transfer to developing countries. Consequently, the process of industrialization in many developing countries can be more environmentally friendly than it was in today's industrial countries.

New Political Developments

Finally, substantial new political developments have taken place since the collapse of communism and the breakup of the bipolar world order. The most significant recent advance in political terms is the great increase in the number of relatively pluralistic and democratic regimes. Closely linked with this is a trend that has developed since the fall of the Berlin Wall: As a result of the change in the global political climate, "good governance" has now become an important topic on the international development policy agenda. Procedures and control mechanisms concerned with good governance are increasingly being included in policy dialogue.

The role of the state in development is now seen in a completely different light than it was in the seventies. Whereas the state was earlier regarded as the driving force in development and the creator of wealth, today it is perceived as having only a catalytic function. The role of the state in promoting sustainable development is now seen as one of facilitation, encouragement, and the creation of conditions in which individuals and private enterprises can develop and flourish on their own.[6] By the same logic, efforts at institutional development and capacity building no longer focus only on public institutions but also on the private sector and nongovernmental organizations.

Global demilitarization continues apace. Military spending reached a historic high point in 1984, with total expenditures of $1,140 billion, but by 1996 it had dropped by 39 percent, to approximately $700 billion (in 1995 dollars). The number of armed conflicts declined from 50 in 1992 to 24 in 1998.[7]

The status of women and relations between the sexes have also become leading concerns of development policy and are now increasingly included in projects and programs focusing on the role of women.

What Remains to Be Done

Progress has not occurred everywhere, nor has it by any means affected everyone.[8] The people of an entire continent—Africa—have barely shared in the progress just described. Rather, the combined impacts of poverty, poor government, scarce water and land resources, and high rates of population growth translate into a major setback for many African countries. The United Nations Development Programme projects that it will take two generations for the people of sub-Saharan Africa to reach the standard of living of the world as a whole during the mid-seventies.

Social Deprivation

The difference in life expectancy between the richest and the poorest countries is still almost 45 years.[9] Women in Japan had an average life expectancy of 84 in 1999, and most women in Western and Southern Europe now have life expectancies exceeding 80. People in many countries of sub-Saharan Africa, however, can only expect to reach about the age of 40. According to the World Bank database, life expectancy at birth in many poor countries in sub-Saharan Africa remains at 40–45 years. Three of every four people in the world's poorest countries die before they turn 50.[10]

Child mortality is still 50 times higher in the poorest countries than in the richest. In 1999, the child mortality rate in Sweden was 3.6 per 1,000 live births. In countries with the highest rates of child mortality, this figure was well above 130; in the Western Sahara it exceeded 150. According to UNICEF more than 30,000 children under the age of five continue to die each day from a wide variety of causes; some sources put this figure as high as 40,000.[11]

More than 840 million people in the world are still illiterate, and approximately two thirds of them are women and girls. Roughly 130 million school-age children do not attend school.

There are still stark contrasts between the rights and duties of men and women and striking differences in the well-being of each sex. If normal statistical distribution of men and women is taken as a basis, there is a "shortage" of almost 100 million women in developing countries, owing to neglect of newborn and unwanted baby girls, as well as other forms of social discrimination. Moreover, widespread economic disparities between men and women continue to exist.

Food insecurity is very much a developing-country phenomenon: less than 5 percent of the 824 million food-insecure people worldwide live in industrial countries. Indeed, 18 percent of the people in the developing world are considered food-insecure. The situation is particularly dire in sub-Saharan Africa, which is the only region where the number of food-insecure people has increased in the last 25 years. It is also the only region where the number of malnourished has increased since 1970, where per capita food production has declined since the early sixties, and where the food available per person through production plus imports has been virtually unchanged.

Even where caloric intakes are adequate, many people suffer from hidden hunger in the form of micronutrient deficiencies due to poor diets. Worldwide, about 2 billion people suffer from iron-deficiency anemia, more than 2 billion are at risk of iodine-deficiency disorders, and 250 million children are affected by severe vitamin A deficiency.

Economic Deprivation

Economic polarization has increased markedly throughout the world in the last 30 years.[12] The richest 20 percent of Earth's inhabitants saw their share of world income rise from 70 to 85 percent in this period, while the share of the poorest 20 percent declined from 2.3 to 1.4 percent. The total assets of the world's 358 billionaires amounted to more than the combined gross national products of the world's developing countries, where 45 percent of the world now lives.

Disparities within individual societies also increased. Virtually all developing and industrial countries were affected—not just the United States.[13] This phenomenon was partly due to high rates of unemployment and underemployment. The future dimensions of the employment problem are enormous: according to conservative estimates made by the Organisation for Economic Co-operation and Development, 1 billion jobs will have to be created worldwide in the next 10 years to absorb first-time job seekers.[14]

The income gap between industrial and developing countries widened from $5,700 to $17,000 between 1960 and 1997. Since the early nineties, per capita incomes have dropped by 20 percent and more in many countries (primarily in Eastern Europe and the former Soviet Union). As a result of the Asian financial crisis, more than 50 million people in some countries (Indonesia, for example) sank into absolute poverty, which had previously been sharply reduced there.

Approximately 1.3 billion people—almost one third of the people in developing countries—live in absolute poverty on less than $1 a day (in terms of 1985 purchasing power). Another 2 billion people must get by on less than $2 a day.[15] In other words, half of humanity currently exists or tries to exist on $2 a day or less.

Ecological Threats

Use of renewable resources—land, forests, fresh water, coastal areas, fishing grounds, and air—has now exceeded the capacity for regeneration in many regions.[16] (See Chapter 4 for further discussion of these trends.) Global energy consumption is not sustainable at current levels: since 1971 it has risen almost 70 percent and, if current projections are accurate, it will rise more than 2 percent annually for the next 15 years.[17] Less than one fourth of the people in the world consume three quarters of Earth's natural resources and produce 70 percent of all solid waste.[18]

Global emissions of greenhouse gases are still higher than the target level set by international agreement. Since the United Nations Conference on Environment and Development in Rio de Janeiro in 1992, global carbon dioxide emissions have risen by 4 percent; the concentration of carbon dioxide in the atmosphere has now reached its highest level in 160,000 years.[19] In fact, 1998 was the warmest year since average atmospheric temperature measurements were first made in 1866, and the nineties was the warmest decade on record.[20]

One hectare of forest disappears every two seconds; human settlements and newly cleared agricultural land are encroaching on protected areas and tropical forestland, and contributing to loss of biodiversity. In 1997, forest fires in Indonesia and the Amazon region caused widespread damage.[21]

Global consumption of water is accelerating. In the near future, water shortages are likely to be the greatest single development problem and represent one of the largest potential threats among sources of armed conflict. Drastic shortages already exist: in 1997 so much water was diverted from the upper reaches of the Yellow River in China that it failed to flow to the China Sea for 226 days of the year.[22]

More than 1.5 billion people still have no access to clean water, and 2 billion have no access to proper wastewater disposal. More than 1.5 billion people are forced to live with air pollution that is a threat to their health, and over 500 million have no alternative but to live in ecologically fragile regions.[23] Acid rain is posing a growing problem in Asia. If present trends continue, it is forecast that emissions of sulfur dioxide will triple in the next 10 years.[24]

Political Shortcomings

From a political perspective, the world has not yet reached the "end of history" that was widely discussed after the breakup of the Soviet Union.[25] As this book was being written, a gruesome war was raging in Kosovo; shortly before, commissioners of the European Union were forced to step down under accusations of corruption. Whatever we may lament about the political shortcomings in developing countries, there are no islands of paradise in the industrial world.

Inept government remains the greatest hindrance to sustainable development in many nations. Despite improvements in the art of governance, countless millions of people are still the victims of repression and violence for ethnic, religious, or political reasons. The annual reports of Amnesty International continue to document political repression in practically every country in the world.

With few exceptions, the financial crisis of the welfare state is still unresolved. Owing to struggles among various social groups to defend their vested interests, most industrial countries are not in a position to undertake necessary political reforms and structural adjustments. And global structures of governance and global solidarity with regard to social and ecological issues have not yet developed sufficiently for common progress in these areas to become a reality.[26]

Figure 3   Urban and Rural Shares of World Population, 1950–2030

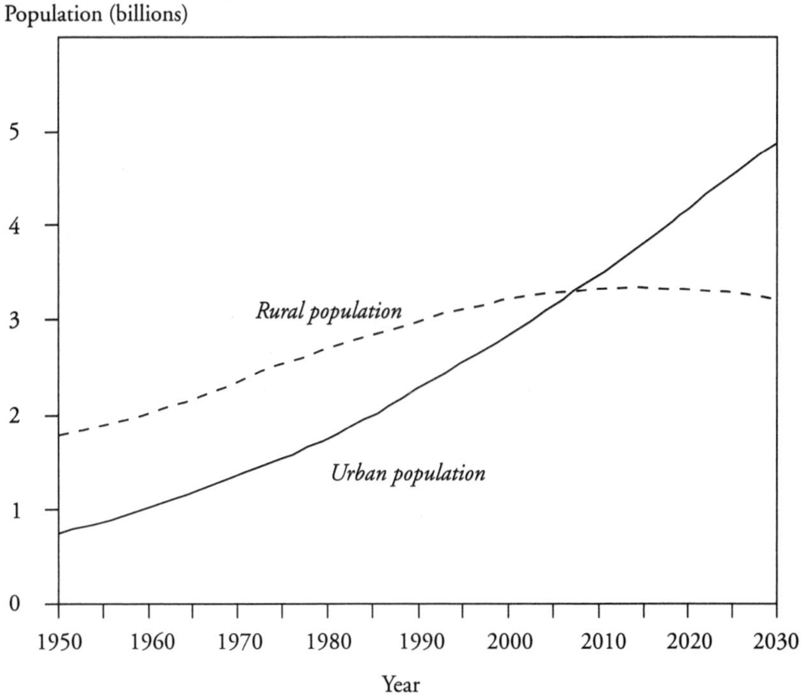

Population (billions)

Year

Source: United Nations Population Division, *World Urbanization Prospects: The 1999 Revision* (New York, 2000).

Worrying Demographic Developments

Three recent demographic trends may color the world's future success in achieving food security and sustainable development for a growing population: rapid urbanization, aging populations, and the speedy spread of HIV. These three developments, along with other uncertainties, offer sufficient reason to consider the accuracy of projections about the future.

Urbanization

The start of the twenty-first century marks the first time in human history that more people are living in cities and towns than in rural areas (see Figure 3). A near doubling of the world's urban population is expected between 1995 and 2030, from 2.6 billion to 4.9 billion people, nearly 4 billion of whom will live in developing countries.[27] More than half the population of Africa and Asia will be urban by 2020; more than three quarters of Latin Americans already are.[28]

China and India epitomize the huge shifts under way.[29] While two out of three Chinese currently live in rural areas, the country is expected to become predominantly urban by 2030. And by then some 600 million people are likely to be living in cities in India—about the same as the combined population of Japan, Russia, and the United States. Given current trends, it can be assumed that the population in rural regions in developing countries overall will decline after 2015.

Rapid urban population growth is confronting people in cities and local authorities with problems of historically new dimensions. Recent migrants have limited resources with which to meet their needs. They are conscious of being culturally uprooted and suffer from a lack of security provided by the extended family and the ethnic or religious community. If they find work at all, it is usually in the form of insecure and poorly paid jobs in the informal sector. Thus a shift of the impoverished population away from rural areas will go hand-in-hand with urbanization. Garrett notes that both the proportion and the number of poor people living in urban areas grew during the eighties and nineties in seven out of eight countries surveyed, including India and China.[30] Similarly, from the early to the mid-nineties, the urban share of malnourished children rose in 15 countries for which data are available.[31]

Urban poverty has a direct impact on the health of poor people in cities. Most new immigrants to the cities cannot afford a decent place to live and are therefore forced to stay with others in crowded quarters with no proper sanitation or access to basic services. Infectious diseases of all kinds can spread easily. Social upheaval has led to the explosive growth of AIDS in cities. In many cases the mortality rate by age group in cities exceeds the rate in rural areas.

Rapid urbanization also undermines food security. People living in cities cannot feed themselves by subsistence farming. They must purchase most of their food, so their food security depends on what they can afford to buy. Thus food security in urban areas is inextricably linked to income security.

Moreover, urban dwellers have different dietary habits than people in rural areas. As people move to cities, their diets shift away from coarse grains such as sorghum and millet to rice, and sometimes then to wheat. They tend to eat greater amounts of livestock products and more processed, transportable, storable foods. They also consume more fat, and their diets tend to contain animal proteins rather than plant proteins. Thus it is not surprising that increasing urbanization in the developing world has been accompanied by a higher incidence of obesity and of diabetes and coronary problems, even though undernutrition and poverty-related diseases remain major problems.[32]

These new eating patterns require higher levels of cereal production (for animal fodder) and greater amounts of agricultural land devoted to grazing. Even today the approximately 400 million small-scale farmers in developing countries are unable to supply urban populations with enough food. How, then, will it be possible for 800 million small-scale farmers to supply over 4 billion city dwellers in 2020?

As long as governments continue to direct the lion's share of development support to cities at the expense of rural areas, people will continue to abandon their original homes—a point that is made time and again in official policy recommendations. Policymakers will need to deal with both "pull" and "push" factors if they are to bring the process of urbanization under control.

Aging Populations

Never before in human history have so many people become so old. Today more than 600 million people have passed their sixtieth birthday, and the generation that is now over 70 is growing at a rate previously unknown in human history. In parts of Canada, Europe, Japan, and the United States, the proportion of people between the ages of 65 and 79 is growing faster than any other age group.[33] If birth rates and mortality rates continue on this path, almost 20 percent of the world will be over the age of 60 by mid-century (see Figure 4).

Where fertility rates are generally lower (primarily in Australia, Europe, Japan, North America, and New Zealand), the proportion of people over the age of 65 will double in the next 30–35 years, rising to 40 percent and more in countries such as Germany, where populations are aging most rapidly. In some countries the number of people over 85 will double within the same period.

Surprisingly, populations in developing regions of the world are also aging. Currently, developing countries account for about 80 percent of the increase in the number of the people in the world between the ages of 65 and 79. By mid-century, all of the growth in this predominately female age group will be in developing countries.

The proportion of people of working age will decline markedly in comparison to the proportion of people receiving old-age assistance. This shift will create numerous difficulties in the funding of social security systems and in covering the costs of health care and nursing care. It will be particularly difficult to solve problems related to old age where large families are breaking up under the influence of modernization and no reliable system of public assistance exists. Although people now live longer and remain healthier than ever before, countries with aging populations will be confronted by completely different and probably more expensive health problems than in the past.

Figure 4   World Population Age 60 and Older and Age 80 and Older, 1950–2050

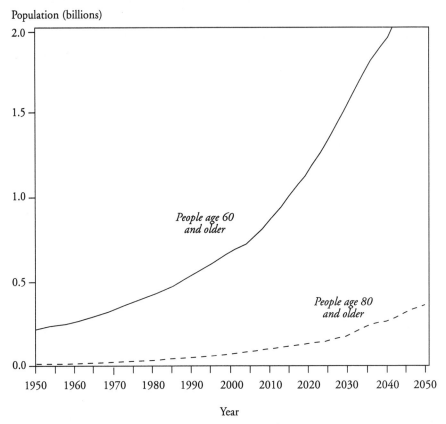

Source: United Nations Population Division, Department of Economic and Social Affairs, *World Population Prospects: The 1998 Revision*, Vol. II: *The Sex and Age Distribution of the World Population* (New York, 1999).

This "graying" of the world's population also has important implications for agriculture. First, different age groups have different nutritional needs. In India, for instance, over the next half-century the caloric requirements for those under the age of five are expected to decline, while those of individuals age 60 and older are due to increase by 250 percent.[34] A second effect is due to the disproportionate aging of the farming population in many developing countries. Young people in rural areas are more apt to move to "the big city," even in industrial countries. The average age of farmers in Japan, for example, is 60, and in the United States it is 57.[35] Experience shows that many of these older farmers in developing nations will be marginal producers, requiring government subsidies and protection, if available, and thereby reducing the nation's food security.[36]

HIV/AIDS

AIDS is the third recent worrying demographic development. No other epidemic since the great Chinese famine of 1959–61, which claimed 30 million lives, appears to have decimated human beings with enough force to cause a measurable decline in population growth. AIDS now claims more human lives worldwide than any other infectious disease, and it has become the number one killer in Africa.[37]

According to the World Health Organization (WHO), 36 million people had HIV/AIDS as of late 2000. A dramatic rise in mortality will occur if no significant breakthroughs are achieved in research on curative and preventive measures—specifically, development of a vaccination against infection, since the use of condoms and safe sex practices that would prevent unwanted pregnancies as well as sexually transmitted diseases and HIV infection is not widespread. Moreover, any curative and preventive measures will have to be available at affordable prices.

AIDS has eradicated a great deal of progress in health and development. Today it is reducing the life expectancy of the adult population in virtually every country in sub-Saharan Africa. In Botswana, where 36 percent of adults are HIV-positive, life expectancy at birth will drop to about 37 within the next few years; in the absence of the AIDS epidemic, it would now be about 70. Indeed, as a result of AIDS, Botswana's population will barely grow between now and 2050, and it may even decline—despite a high birth rate.

AIDS also has a direct impact on people's ability to acquire enough nutritious food to lead active, healthy lives. It affects the availability of labor to work the farms and can force people to reallocate their scarce household resources from agriculture to patient care. When the disease takes adults in rural areas, it can leave orphans and the elderly, who may lack the experience or the strength to continue farming. The ripple effects of this devastating illness in terms of food security are considerable: it can alter the crops people plant as they shift, for example, to fast-maturing but less profitable root crops, and it can force farmers to sell income-producing animals to cover health care costs or even to slaughter livestock for consumption during funerals.[38]

In its recently revised projections, the United Nations Population Division took explicit account of the higher mortality rate from AIDS and made a downward adjustment in its figures for the year 2050.

Two Views of the Population Problem

The facts and trends just described may be subject to general agreement, but their implications are not. Antithetical views on the future exist side by side, as they have for centuries. In 1750 Johann Peter Süssmilch, a Berlin vicar and statistician, estimated that Earth could feed at least 10 billion people. But some 50 years later,

Süssmilch's English colleague, Thomas Robert Malthus, foretold a black future.[39] The current protagonists in the debate are Julian Simon in one corner versus Paul and Anne Ehrlich and Lester Brown in the other. According to the publications of the Ehrlichs or Lester Brown, the global community is adopting the lemming approach.[40] Yet the writings of Julian Simon or Ronald Bailey paint a bright, rosy future.[41] According to the cover text of Julian Simon's last book, "All trends in material affluence for human beings have improved—and that will remain so in the future, since advances in technology and new research findings will provide a completely new framework for future actions."[42]

The interested layperson remains frustratingly unenlightened—how can anyone come to an informed opinion on such a complex issue if gifted scientists can arrive at such different conclusions based on the same data? Answering this question involves dividing the world roughly into two camps—pessimists and optimists—and examining their methods. The first thing to notice is that the statements of pessimists and optimists are based on different value judgments and methodologies.

In many cases—though not all—pessimists take an actual set of conditions and extrapolate the most important trends of the past into the future. Model assumptions are based on the principle of *ceteris paribus*—that is, "other things being equal." Individual problem areas (such as current stocks of natural oil) are picked out from the complex mosaic of the economic, political, social, and ecological world. These are compared with the current consumption trend and used as a basis to calculate what would happen if the trend were to continue, other things being equal.

Let us assume that current natural oil stocks amount to 100 million units and that current consumption is 4 million units a year. All other things being equal, the volume of natural oil will last the current world population 25 years. Assuming more realistically that consumption will increase because of industrialization and motorization in developing countries and that population will increase, the availability period for oil declines dramatically. Asked whether new natural oil stocks might be discovered, pessimists reply in the positive but qualify this by citing the increasing environmental costs required to extract oil (in mud flats, for instance, or Alaska or the Amazon), so that ultimately more is lost in environmental terms than is gained in terms of raw resources. The same thinking is applied to all other nonrenewable resources. Technical modifications (the two-liter car) or innovative production methods (oil from coal) are regarded by pessimists as feasible but as a temporary postponement of inevitable and imminent disaster. Technological advances that increase resource productivity are often judged to be negligible since they are more than offset by the quantitative effect of unchanged behavior patterns.

The underlying psychological tendency of pessimistic models is mostly negative, partly moralistic, and in almost all cases in favor of stronger state intervention. Pessimists define "sustainable development" as a relatively static concept—that is, future generations should be assured a comparable capital stock of natural resources for the purposes of satisfying their needs. From this point of view, any consumption of natural resource stocks is therefore problematic; only the consumption of the "interest" on natural capital would be legitimate. The assumption that innovations could increase Earth's available natural capital and that the requisite investments of natural capital would be justified is given short shrift. Most pessimists believe that the state and its command-and-control mechanisms are important elements in seeking ways out of the crisis.

Pessimists conclude thus: the end of the world is nigh—at least the end of the current production, consumption, and waste culture. We must therefore turn our backs on technology, with its empty promises of efficiency, embrace self-sacrifice, and limit our consumption to the level of subsistence.

Optimists like Julian Simon think completely differently. They do not assume "other things being equal" since the real world is shaped by circular interdependencies, and inventiveness promises endless innovation. In other words, nothing stays as it is, since people respond intelligently to changing circumstances, conflicts, and scarcities. Intensive research will produce new findings and an infinite array of technical innovations, thus preventing distribution conflicts between present and future generations. Thanks to ongoing advances in knowledge and technology, everything we regard as "sustainable" based on our present level of knowledge and in the light of our current interests will be irrelevant for future generations. Even as recently as the sixties, the top managers of some large electronic companies believed the development of small computers for personal use was impossible, and the idea of mobile telephones and the Internet was confined to the pages of science fiction books.

For Julian Simon, it is not raw materials per se that are valuable for the quality of human life, but the services they enable. If fiber-optic telecommunications become cheaper or better, the scarcity of copper loses significance. If goods formerly manufactured from light metals serve the same purpose if made from composite materials, or if iron is replaced by ceramics and other such substitutions are possible, the scarcity of natural raw materials is less meaningful.

Optimists also believe the negative impact of scarcity on society is short-term only. In their view, the longer-term impact is positive, since it acts as an incentive to innovate and substitute and galvanizes human inventiveness. For this school of thought, any progress is a natural adaptive response to a concrete scarcity and not merely a happy coincidence.

The fundamental psychological tendency of the "optimist" model is forward-looking, competitive, and generally in opposition to state intervention. Conflicts of interest and the search for individual material benefits are valued as the driving forces of social progress. This is particularly true of democratic societies with healthy market economies and intensive competition, where individuals have the freedom to develop. Regulations aimed at environmental protection are regarded as administrative overkill.

Optimists define sustainable development as a dynamic concept and strive to provide future generations not with the same stock of natural resources but with comparable options. The consumption of natural resources is not a problem, provided it fuels innovation and allows future generations to enjoy a high quality of life. Hence the optimists' message: don't worry, resources are there to be used; every generation should consume as much as it wants. What society needs is economic growth. This is only achievable by using resources. Today's resource consumption is an investment in future earnings; curbing consumption now would obstruct progress for future generations.

However counterintuitive and out of touch with the *Zeitgeist* they seem to be, the arguments of the optimistic school of thought carry too much weight to be simply swept aside. So we must ask ourselves: in our attempt to achieve sustainable development, are we confronting inevitable forces? Or are the problems we face based on processes that can be influenced by human inventiveness and technical progress?

Chapter 2

From Population Theory to Reality

The first forecast made by U.N. population experts in 1951 projected a global population of 3.3 billion by 1981. The actual figure was 4.4 billion.[1] In the early nineties, forecasts of global population by 2100 projected a maximum of 14.1 billion and a minimum of approximately 8 billion. The difference, slightly more than 6 billion, is roughly the number of people alive today.[2] What is the use of such wide-ranging and even mistaken forecasts?

In examining population projections, it is important to remember that they are not predictions of definite developments; they indicate the number of people a country or a region will have if the economic, social, ecological, and political assumptions that underlie the forecasts remain valid. In other words, they provide a hypothetical statistical scenario. The inaccuracy of the 1951 projection, for example, was partly the result of insufficient knowledge about the population of China at that time and partly the result of pessimistic assumptions about the decline of infant and child mortality in developing countries.

The most important factors influencing the future population of a country are

- current population and age structure,

- assumed birth rate,[3]

- assumed life expectancy, and

- the amount of time projected until population growth stabilizes.[4]

Which U.N. forecasts will turn out to be accurate when we bear in mind that the funds for population programs will not be available in the amounts pledged in

1994 at the International Conference on Population and Development in Cairo? No one can answer this question at the moment.

Population forecasts beyond a particular point in time are of limited value. We cannot forecast economic, social, ecological, and technological conditions at the middle of the twenty-first century, nor do we know the long-term impact of AIDS on, say, the population of sub-Saharan Africa. Demographer Nathan Keyfitz has described the problem of population forecasting in these terms:

> Demographers can no more be held responsible for inaccurate forecasts of population 20 years into the future than geologists, meteorologists, or economists can be held responsible for their failure to predict earthquakes, cold winters, or economic crises 20 years in advance.[5]

Nevertheless, forecasts of demographic developments play a useful and important role in forming the basis of policy recommendations.

In general, forecasts inspire considerable public reaction. We do not know whether the world's population will eventually level off at 9, 10, or 11 billion. Forecasts made by the World Bank in 1984 varied by as much as 3 billion, depending on whether they were based on favorable or unfavorable assumptions. Today, there is general agreement that world population will reach about 8.9 billion by 2050. But no one can be certain of that.

The great weakness in making population forecasts can be traced to calculations that are inaccurate because they are based only on demographic indicators. Ecological bottlenecks—such as water scarcity (in the Middle East and North Africa, for example) or shortages of land (in China, for instance)—are given as little consideration as social catastrophes such as war. In the same way, current forecasts casually ignore such problems as climate change or further depletion of the ozone layer. Yet forecasts made without taking ecological conditions into account can reveal astounding shortcomings when we consider the fate of people in the Sahel zone of Africa, where, among other things, there is a lack of food security resulting from drought.

Assumptions about social conditions and political decisions also have a major influence on population forecasts. Will China continue to pursue its present population policies, or will it change course and, if so, in what direction? Will the birth rate in sub-Saharan Africa really decline as soon as modernization takes permanent root in traditional African societies? Will the increase in mortality owing to AIDS make it impossible to conduct family-planning campaigns? Or will the spread of this disease make condom use more acceptable? How will people in Indonesia respond to growing poverty resulting from financial crisis? Will they decide to have fewer children until the crisis has passed, as people in the United States and Europe did during the Great Depression in the early twentieth century? Or will they follow the traditional pattern of poor societies and respond to rising mortality rates by having more children?

Different answers to these questions, as well as errors in making assumptions, influence the results of population forecasts and account for variations among them. If forecasts are based on good social data, desirable population policy decisions, and the assumptions of individual initiative, the result will be a "low" figure for global population. If the opposite holds true, the results are bound to show a "high" figure.

Carl Haub, senior demographer at the Population Reference Bureau, has cited three criteria that can be used as a rule of thumb in population forecasting.[6] A population forecast is more realistic

- the shorter its time frame,

- the larger the geographical area for which it is made, and

- the lower the current birth rates and the higher the current life expectancy of people in the area covered by the forecast.

Forecasts that cover short periods of time, such as 10 years, reflect observations of the recent past. This reduces the chance of error to a relative minimum, as age structure, mortality rates, birth rates, and possible migration patterns are known. Forecasts for an entire continent are likely to be more accurate than those for a single country, since overestimates, underestimates, and other errors may balance out. In the final analysis, countries with high birth and death rates have a much greater potential for demographic change than those with low fertility and mortality rates. At least the last of the three criteria mentioned suggests that population forecasts for developing countries are more likely to be in error than those for industrial nations.

The undeniable value of population forecasts lies in the fact that they can indicate trends under certain conditions, as well as the possible consequences of these trends. They offer a chance to take appropriate corrective action with respect to certain developments—the opportunity need only be seized. In the view of the philosopher Hans Jonas, the aim and the purpose of prophecies of disaster is to provoke change and, by so doing, to be proved wrong.[7]

The Population Factor

It is one thing to know roughly how many people will be living on Earth at a particular moment in the future. But how do we determine the point at which the population of a particular region or country, or indeed the globe, will become too big?

It has been known for centuries that the world's population is growing. More-over, the consequences of this growth were described as early as the Middle Ages. We know as well that it is not only the number of people living in a country or a region that is important but the ways in which they live, their forms of social organization, and their consumption patterns. The importance of the "population factor" becomes clear only in relation to economic development (and thus to per capita consumption), the characteristics of development policy in a particular country (and thus the social, economic, and political environment), the supply of natural resources, the level of technology (and thus eco-efficiency), and cultural conditions.

For example, "too little" population growth leads to great difficulties in the financing of social security systems, while at the same time "too many" children in sub-Saharan Africa will make it difficult for African schools to maintain quality. Only when population data are "relativized" in the light of individual value judgments is it possible to draw conclusions about such things as "overpopulation" or "overly slow population growth."

Some regions (such as the Sahel) are already overpopulated in relation to available resources and would thus need to experience a negative rate of growth to improve the quality of life. Other societies that are rich in natural resources are unlikely to have problems in the foreseeable future, even though some have rates of population growth above 2 percent. If agricultural potential were the only criterion used to gauge optimal population levels, countries such as Malaysia or the Congo could support three to four times as many people. In general, the concept of "overpopulation" applies only when available natural resources are being overexploited or when available capital is inadequate to make the investments necessary for a decent quality of life—even in the case of lifestyles based on subsistence agriculture.[8]

Yet a population may also be considered "too small" and its rate of growth regarded as "too slow." Hundreds of millions of people live in conditions so miserable that they claim the life of one in three children before the age of five. When parents depend on children in the absence of public or other institutional health and social security systems under such conditions, even four or five children often provide too little social security for parents. And in cultures where girls join their husband's families at the time of betrothal and are thus no longer available to care for their own parents in old age, four children may be too few for old-age security if they are "only" girls.

Finally, a country with a very low population density and an abundance of fertile land may find itself envied—sometimes mildly, sometimes aggressively, but envied nonetheless—by a neighboring country that is armed to the teeth and suffering from a shortage of land in light of its rapidly growing population. The former country's government may conclude under such circumstances that its own population is "too small" and that a higher rate of population growth would enhance its geopolitical position and the long-term security of its population.

We do not know how many people are too many for Earth overall. But there are growing social and ecological indications that sustainable development will not be possible for everyone if population growth rates remain high. Yet the same indications can be found on the other side of the coin: sustainable development will also be impossible if the richest 10–15 percent of the world's population continues its current high level of energy and resource consumption. If everyone in the world had the same standard of living as the Indians of the Brazilian rain forest, Earth could support 20–30 billion people. But if everyone consumed resources at the same level as the inhabitants of the United States, Earth's carrying capacity would already have been exceeded today.

The relationship between population growth and human development is extremely complex and can by no means be traced to one cause. Proof of this can be found in the fact that the global population of just over 6 billion in 2001 is considerably better off than the population of 3 billion who were alive in 1960.

Understanding Patterns of Population Growth

Theorists have advanced a number of ideas concerning the factors that encourage or limit population growth in the past couple of centuries. In 1798, Thomas Robert Malthus published his *Essay on the Principle of Population As It Affects the Future Improvement of Society*.[9] This systematic discussion of the impacts of population growth on human welfare and national economic development, which went through seven subsequent editions, with slight revisions over time, was based on the fact that a population whose growth is "unrestricted" will increase in geometric progression (or 1, 2, 4, 8, 16, and so on). Malthus pointed out that human beings exist within a finite space and that annual increases in the food supply depend upon improvement of arable land already in use. Based on his assessment of global conditions, Malthus concluded that even the most assiduous human effort could do no more than increase the food supply in arithmetic progression (1, 2, 3, 4, 5, and so on).[10]

According to Malthus, an overly high rate of population growth would also pose a threat to stable political development, since hunger and the suffering born of poverty would be the source of endless political upheaval and carnage.[11] This conclusion has some relevance to the conditions found in numerous countries today.

Many aspects of Malthus's theory have been disputed since his time. But his hypotheses are still of interest with regard to the impact of high population growth on aggregate material resources.

The Law of the Minimum, formulated more than a century ago by Justus von Liebig, states that the yield of a particular species is proportional to the amount of the most limiting nutrient, whatever that may be. We do not know just what "nutrient" will turn out to be the limiting one for humans—water, air, land, or the protective atmospheric boundary layer. In light of the knowledge we have today, however, we do know that many important natural resources are finite in quantity, at least in the long term. As Malthus perceived in his day, we could still face the problem of a widening gulf between two dynamic limiting factors—increasing population and a decreasing natural resource base—unless this can be prevented through further social and technological innovations resulting from human ingenuity.

Recommendations on population policy and programs concerned with reproductive health in developing countries are often based expressly or indirectly on the assumption that developing countries will undergo a "demographic transition," just as industrial countries did over the last 200 years. Such a transition has a minimum of three phases, from a "traditional society" that has high rates of birth and mortality and low population growth, to a "modern society" with low birth and mortality rates and declining population growth.[12] Between these two conditions there is a "transition phase" in which mortality has already dropped but the birth rate is still high, resulting in high population growth.

The demographic transition theory gained popularity in the fifties during debates about strategies of population policy for developing countries. The widespread attention given to the theory was based partly on its apparently obvious plausibility and partly on a contemporary view according to which the process of development was overwhelmingly understood in terms of developing countries "catching up" with industrial countries. The temptation and the potential for error involved in making demographic forecasts for developing countries from the socioeconomic perspective of industrial ones was recognized early, and appropriate warnings were issued.[13] There was agreement that the theory of demographic transition was merely a general model of change in birth and death rates resulting from social change. There was never a serious body of opinion maintaining that the theory constituted a "law" that could be applied to other periods of time and other societies and cultures. This is still true today.

The theory is not precise enough to make exact forecasts about the duration of transition phases or to specify other quantifiable social and economic thresholds beyond which the birth rate will begin to drop. In any case, there are no "magic numbers" for threshold levels of industrialization, gross domestic product, or literacy. There is still no consensus today about the relative importance of specific factors that influence the transition or about which indicators (such as income distribution) should be considered and which can be ignored.

It is important to note that the demographic transition in Europe was highly uneven in both duration and structure and cannot be analyzed in simple terms. Individual countries in pre-modern Europe exhibited pronounced regional deviations. In addition, in some cases birth rates declined before modernization set in and in others they remained high even after the beginning of modernization. Studies by Paul Demeny and, later, by Ansley Coale have brought to light developments that remain unexplained: in numerous societies of pre-modern Europe, there was no decline in mortality rates before the decline in fertility. Rather, both rates declined simultaneously. And in France as well as several provinces of Germany, birth rates even declined before death rates.[14]

Still, it has been argued that what is traditionally thought of as the "European pattern" of demographic transformation—from high birth and death rates through a transition phase and then to low birth and death rates—could be applied to developing countries today. But there are also counterarguments, according to which the demographic transformation of Europe was a historically and culturally unique phenomenon.

Numerous differences distinguish Europe in the eighteenth and nineteenth centuries from today's developing countries: There were fewer than 200 million people in Europe when the transition began, whereas today the population of the developing world is nearly 5 billion.[15] Crude birth rates are higher today in these nations than they were in pre-modern Europe. Doubling times are very different—it would have taken Europe 150 years to double its population at the nineteenth-century growth rate, compared with about 24 years for all of West Africa today. In addition, migration cannot serve as the escape valve that it did for the British, Italians, Spaniards, and others nearly 200 years ago.

Marital age and frequency of marriage are also areas in which important differences can be found between traditional European societies and today's developing countries. In pre-modern Europe, strict cultural norms and social codes kept the marital age for women relatively high—much higher, in any case, than in traditional societies in the South today.

The general decline in mortality rates has also followed a different course. In Europe, rising standards of living and improvements in sanitation, hygiene, and diet, as well as higher levels of education and training, were responsible for a continual decline in mortality rates over approximately 150 years. Today, developing countries can import vaccines, medicine, and chemicals for vector control from industrial countries and put them to widespread use with the help of international development organizations, regardless of their level of modernization. This has allowed a substantial "imported" reduction in mortality, especially among infants and children, within only a few years. The infant mortality rate alone declined from an average of 140 per 1,000 births in 1960 to approximately 70 in 1999.

At the same time, however, mortality rates have remained unstable in many countries owing to the disruptions of war, political and economic chaos, and misguided governmental priorities. As long as infant and child mortality continues at high levels, parents will continue to regard children as the only reliable source of security in old age, as well as a source of other economic and social benefits. They will not be prepared to reduce the number of children they have until they are convinced it is reasonable to do so.

Finally, and quite important, given current high levels of social and ecological stress, developing countries do not have the luxury of 150–200 years in which to complete the demographic transition, as European nations did.

To balance the points just made, a few arguments have been advanced in favor of applying the European model of demographic transition to today's developing countries. First, where the quality of life improves, mortality rates decline. When a society is at peace and can meet its basic needs on a sustainable basis, it will first experience a decline in the rate of infant mortality. This is the most sensitive indicator of the quality of human life.

Second, birth rates decline more slowly than mortality rates. The same reasons that led to a continuance of high birth rates at a time of declining mortality rates during the intermediate phase of European demographic transition apply to developing countries today. Traditional patterns of thought and behavior, moral and religious codes, and a series of other influencing factors that vary from culture to culture are slowing down the decline in birth rates in proportion to mortality rates. This can be seen in a comparison of relative declines in crude birth and death rates (see Table 3).

Table 3   Relative Changes in Crude Birth and Death Rates, 1960–99

	Death rate			Birth rate		
	Deaths per 1,000 population			Births per 1,000 population		
Country or countries	1960	1999	Change (percent)	1960	1999	Change (percent)
Mali	30	16	−46.6	50	47	−0.6
Uganda	21	19	−9.6	49	48	−2.0
India	22	9	−59.1	44	28	−36.4
China	14	6	−57.1	40	16	−60.0
All developing countries	26	9	−65.4	48	26	−45.8

Source: Data for 1960 from World Bank, *World Development Report 1978* (New York: Oxford University Press, 1978); data for 1999 from Population Reference Bureau, *1999 World Population Data Sheet* (Washington, DC: 1999).

The logical consequence is the high population growth that has persisted roughly since the end of World War II, bearing out the predictions made by those who developed the demographic transition theory. Population policy since the war has aimed to accelerate the decline in birth rates—in other words, to induce the third phase of demographic transition—an effort that has met with some success.

Since the historical process of demographic transition in Europe occurred under social, economic, and demographic conditions remarkably different from conditions in developing countries, it is clear that single explanations are inadequate.[16] A decline in mortality does not by itself necessarily lead to a decline in birth rates, at least not within a period of time that is relevant in development terms.

Today, although urbanization and industrialization are certainly important factors accelerating the process of demographic transition, they are neither necessary nor sufficient to induce it.[17] Some agricultural societies in pre-modern Europe had declining birth rates—just as Sri Lanka and the Indian state of Kerala do today. And some developing countries have experienced a process of demographic transition within a relatively short period that is similar to the European pattern. Early examples include Iran, Viet Nam, South Korea, and China, as well as Chile and Costa Rica.

In any event, the historical model of demographic transition does not provide a reliable basis for making precise forecasts about the future of all developing countries, given their great cultural, social, and religious diversity. It is too approximate, too simple, too mechanical, and too abstract. In light of the many differences between European countries in the eighteenth and nineteenth centuries and developing countries today, we must beware of a naive belief in demographic inevitabilities during the course of economic development. There were no clearly definable or even quantifiable economic or social "thresholds" in pre-modern Europe, nor are there any in the poor countries of the South today.[18] Nevertheless, the demographic transition theory remains useful and helpful in understanding demographic processes.

The validity of the demographic transition model depends on continual social, economic, and ecological improvement, eventually leading to a complete social transformation that brings general improvement in the quality of life. Yet many disturbing contemporary developments give rise to the fear that transformation of this sort will not occur in many countries. Fresh water and arable land are becoming scarce, many countries exhibit extreme shortcomings in the quality of governance, and new problems with vast dimensions (such as climate change) have appeared. In light of these developments, an increasing number of countries are confronted with the danger of falling into a "demographic trap."

The term demographic trap describes a situation in which the circumstances of human life deteriorate to the extent that the conditions that lead to declining birth rates are no longer present. In this case, high population growth and its economic, social, and ecological impacts not only trap people in poverty, they also lead to increased poverty. This in turn produces a rise in mortality, with the result that the society slips back to the first phase of demographic transition. No country can exist permanently in the intermediate phase of transition characterized by high birth rates and low mortality rates. It will either progress toward the third phase or slide back to the first; there are no other options. Lester Brown points to countries such as Afghanistan, Ethiopia, Nigeria, and Sudan as now being directly confronted with this demographic trap.[19] He warns of the possibility that "demographic fatigue" will occur when governments no longer have the necessary resources at their disposal to maintain sustainable processes of development.

Growing unemployment, explosive demands for water, escalating soil degradation, and competition over land are problems whose dimensions have already exceeded manageable proportions, even for governments regarded as competent. New, large-scale problems such as conflict-induced migration, increasingly severe weather-related disasters, outbreaks of new diseases, and the recurrence of age-old diseases such as malaria and tuberculosis are further causes of demographic fatigue that retard development.

Current discussions about population policy focus almost exclusively on the development-inhibiting impacts of high population growth. Some demographers, however, regard population growth—albeit in modest proportions—as highly favorable to a country's economic and social development. Some of these arguments are several decades old and reflect development experience that is now regarded as obsolete. Others, however, were taken up more recently by U.S. authors who developed them further in the eighties.[20]

The pronatalist literature deals primarily with impacts of population growth that are considered positive, including the stimulation of demand, the advantages of mass production, the stimulation of technical progress, incentives for the creation of infrastructure, and a younger population structure, which has certain advantages in terms of the structure of the workforce. Julian Simon, one of the most widely read of the recent pronatalists, viewed human beings as the "ultimate resource."[21] Their creative talents, intelligence, energy, willpower, and imagination can be used to solve problems and secure advantages for themselves and their societies. These strengths enable them to deal with or prevent even the worst disasters. Accordingly, instead of leading to insoluble problems, high population growth may actually represent an opportunity for social development.

This hypothesis is questionable. The sad realities of the crowded slums of Calcutta, Nairobi, Rio de Janeiro, and many other cities today offer little reason to hope that a potential genius will fulfill his or her destiny despite undernourishment in early childhood and a lack of adequate education. It is certainly true that human beings are a source of creative activity and that creative potential is an asset to every society in the North or the South. But before it can flourish and expand, the quality of human life must improve. As long as high rates of population growth persist, this will be a difficult if not impossible task.

Chapter 3

Social and Economic Impacts
of Rapid Population Growth

E very country, region, and family has the capacity for a certain sustainable rate of growth in population. When and where this rate is exceeded varies from one country, region, and family to another, as well as over the course of time. It depends not only on the size of the base population and the available resources (land, capital, raw materials, level of education), but also on the quality of local development policy and the competence of the government and public authorities ("good governance"). Yet once this certain rate of population growth is exceeded, even the best development policy cannot prevent an undesirable impact on the family and on a country's development potential. Nafis Sadik, when she was executive director of the United Nations Population Fund, noted that in many countries the speed of population growth is already outstripping the ability of governments to provide adequate services, social programs, and infrastructures.[1] This situation is akin to trying to run up a down escalator: you have to be very fast to advance even a few steps.

Social Costs at the Family Level
The greatest and most immediate costs of high birth rates are borne by the family, through deterioration in the health of mother and child and added pressures on food supplies.

Health Risks for Mother and Child
Infant, child, and maternal mortality are the social indicators that most clearly reflect the level of poverty in a society. No other indicators reflect the North-South divide so clearly.

At least 500,000 women, 99 percent of whom live in developing countries, die each year as a result of complications arising from pregnancy and birth. This is the equivalent of a jumbo jet with 250 female passengers crashing every four hours a day all year long. Maternal mortality is up to 250 times higher in poor countries than in rich ones.[2]

A large proportion, if not the majority, of maternal deaths can be attributed to undesired pregnancies that could be avoided by family planning. Three quarters of mothers die in childbirth from hemorrhaging, blood poisoning, and birth complications. Another frequent cause of death is backstreet abortions. Of the women who survive these, many suffer lasting damage to their health.[3]

There is a direct, measurable correlation between the health of mother and child, the number of births per woman, the interval between births, and the timing of pregnancies in the life of a woman: the more children a woman bears, the shorter the spacing between births, and the younger (under 18) or older (over 35) a woman is, the worse the health of mother and child and the higher the mortality of both.[4] For biological (physical attributes) as well as societal (economic circumstances and social security) reasons, women under 18, and especially under 16, are exposed to high health risks during pregnancy and birth.[5] For biological reasons, women over 35 are exposed to higher pregnancy and birth-related risks than women in their twenties. Studies in Bangladesh show that 52 percent of maternal deaths in that country could be avoided if women under 20 and over 34 did not become pregnant.[6] If pregnancies ceased after the birth of the fifth child, maternal mortality in Bangladesh would decline by another third.

Exposure to an increased risk of mortality as a result of too-closely-spaced pregnancies is unrelated to domicile (urban or rural), maternal education, or household income—that is, irrespective of the key social indicators used to measure quality of life.[7] But it is especially acute among the lowest-income families and among women whose heavy workload and poor nutritional condition have led to a "wasting" of the body, manifested by iron or vitamin deficiencies, anemia, and other debilitating conditions.[8] Under such harsh conditions, the newborn infant arrives in this world underweight, weak, and sickly and runs a far higher risk of becoming seriously ill and dying before reaching its fifth year.

The social environment of poverty—with high birth rates, lack of hygiene and sanitation, and poor nutrition and housing conditions—significantly endangers the health and survival rates of infants and children under five years old. Infants whose mothers quickly give birth to another child run a particularly high health risk.[9] The same is true of a newborn whose mother has suffered a failed pregnancy or the death of her most recent infant.[10] According to the findings of a Pakistani study, the mortality risk of a child born within two years of a previous pregnancy is 30 percent higher than that of the first-born during the first month of life, 60 percent higher up to the end of the first year, and 50 percent higher up to the end of the fourth year.[11] Infant mortality in many developing countries could be reduced by 20–40 percent if at least two years between births could be achieved through family planning and other means.[12]

Shorter breastfeeding times, premature weaning of infants to solids, and a reduction in the quality of nutrition due to a lower per capita family income (usually as a direct consequence of the growing number of siblings) lead to a deterioration in the nutritional condition of infants.[13] This deterioration is compounded by a decline in the care given to young children following the birth of another child. The new infant receives all the mother's attention, thus marginalizing older siblings in terms of nutrition, hygiene, and general welfare. Generally speaking, the more children there are in a family, the worse their state of health—particularly in the case of younger girls in large families. The opposite case is also well researched and unequivocally proved—that is, the health-related benefits of smaller families.

The key to solving all these problems, besides improving the general living conditions of the poor, lies in better reproductive health. The goal is smaller families and the observance of a reasonable interval (at least 24 months) between pregnancies. This resting period significantly strengthens the condition of mother and child, irrespective of the parents' level of education or place of residence (urban or rural) or the availability of clean drinking water.[14] However, a general improvement in reproductive health cannot be achieved by focusing exclusively on the "female target group." The 1994 International Conference on Population and Development achieved a quantum leap on this issue by examining the role of the male and calling for an increased focus on male responsibility.[15]

Pressures on Food Supplies in Families
Contrary to the popular belief that girls are discriminated against when it comes to food allocation within a household, a comprehensive review finds that with the exception of South Asia, differences between male and female nutritional status are slight.[16] In South Asia, however, females consistently fare worse when it comes to nutritional care. This discrimination has been attributed to the dowry system, which requires families to pay bridegrooms to marry their daughters. Discrimination against girls is not necessarily a feature of the poorest of the poor; in fact, there is considerable evidence that such discrimination is greater in higher-income families. In sub-Saharan Africa, where the culture calls for bridegrooms to pay a bride price, daughters tend to receive better nutritional care than sons. There is little evidence of a pro-male bias in Latin America.

There is also evidence of a pro-adult bias in terms of food intake in South Asia. While this can be partially explained by the tendency of adult males to be engaged in energy-intensive tasks, boys are more favored in terms of food distribution, particularly in the lean season. Other parts of the developing world show less evidence of favoritism toward adults. A number of studies suggest that the first-born child within a family is usually treated well regardless of whether it is male or female. However, later-born girls are more likely to face discrimination relative to their brothers and any older sisters.

Declining Quality of Education

Since all the children in a family must be properly fed, clothed, cared for, and educated, large families incur significantly higher costs than families with fewer children. This forces them to economize on certain aspects of child care. Such cost-cutting is necessarily more drastic in poorer households.

In a study in Colombia, Nancy Birdsall found that the investment per child sinks "monotonously" as the family grows in size.[17] This effect is particularly pronounced if there are five or more children in the family. Since, moreover, less money is available for the younger siblings in a large family (for schooling, educational materials, and the like), educational quality and opportunities deteriorate as the family grows in size.[18] In addition, the duties of caring for younger siblings, imposed primarily on girls, as well as other household chores and child labor all impede school attendance.[19]

The quality of education also declines as a growing cohort of pupils encounters a stagnating number of schoolrooms, teachers, and educational materials. Despite the best intentions, the quality of teaching deteriorates.

In a world increasingly dominated by academic competitiveness, educational deficits—and truly structural deficiencies, such as illiteracy—are the precursors of future unemployment and underemployment, and consequently of poverty.

Disadvantages for the Economy

A recent Worldwatch Institute study, "Nineteen Dimensions of the Population Challenge," addresses many of the social, economic, ecological, and other factors affected by population growth.[20] While it is impossible to discuss here all the problem areas exacerbated by population growth, one fact remains: all problems of underdevelopment are more difficult to resolve if a population has grown rapidly over a number of years.

Back in the early nineties, the United Nations Population Fund conducted a comparative study of 120 countries, examining the impact of high population growth on the performance of national political institutions and the effectiveness of their development policies. The study concluded that very few countries had succeeded, under strong population pressure, "in sustaining stable constitutional conditions with a demonstrable balance of civil and political rights."[21] Moreover, "strong population growth greatly inhibits most governments from keeping pace with growing requirements for health and educational development services."[22] This is still true today.

Reduction in Capital Formation

The total savings volume of a country is the main source of funding for domestic investments. Foreign capital, such as is acquired through development aid or direct foreign investment in a country, normally covers only a small proportion of capital requirements. This poses a problem for countries with rapid population growth, since (as already mentioned) they have a young population, almost half of whom are 14 or younger.

Such a population structure affects the relationship between the employable and unemployable age categories in a population. For example, in 1995 around 68 percent of the population of the German Federal Republic was aged between 15 and 64.[23] Assuming for the sake of argument that all employable persons work until age 65 and that young people enter the job market at age 15 (although actually neither is true today), then 32 percent of the population in 1995 was no longer employable or not yet employable. Similarly, 28.6 percent of the population in Switzerland in 1995 was under 14 or over 64, so 71.4 percent was theoretically employable. All in all, therefore, for every two or more people of working age, there was one person who had to be "supported" by the earnings of others.

The situation is completely different in developing countries with high birth rates. In 1995 around 50 percent of the population of Tanzania was aged between 15 and 64, and similar statistics were recorded for Ethiopia, Burundi, and many other developing countries with low income and high population growth. In other words, around half of the population is either too young or too old to seek gainful employment.[24] If the high level of unemployment and widespread underemployment in most developing countries is taken into account, the actual burden on working age groups is much higher.[25] The young age structure means almost 300 million people will enter the job market over the next two decades. This, coupled with the fact that in some countries the labor force has almost doubled since 1980, is creating employment and social problems on a hitherto unprecedented scale.[26] Moreover, in many countries—particularly in sub-Saharan Africa—agriculture has been incapable of providing enough productive and adequately paid jobs in recent years.[27]

The greater the number of dependents in a family, the more the family must spend on household consumption and the less it is generally able to save and invest.[28] The exact impact on life savings is difficult to determine. Since it can be assumed that children are to some extent an alternative to savings for old age, it is possible to argue that children represent another type of savings capital and to some degree off-set reduced monetary savings. However, the impact of reduced monetary savings at the family level on the economy as a whole substantially weakens overall domestic savings and investment capabilities.[29]

Changes in the Investment Structure

Wherever a population is growing at a rapid pace, permanent investments are required to satisfy the growing demand for public services such as schools, teaching staff, hospitals, health care staff, sanitation, accommodation, jobs, clean water, sewage treatment, and so on. Even now there are many instances of existing capacities being exhausted and administrative structures and authorities overstretched. Strong population growth undermines all efforts to quantitatively or qualitatively improve deficient infrastructures. Many years ago Sir Hans Singer outlined the consequences of high population growth for a nation's investment structure:

> If we compare, say, Great Britain with Kenya, then the size of the labour force in the developed country is growing at a rate of only 0.4 percent and in the developing country at a rate of 3.3 percent. For demographic reasons Kenya must create eight times more employment than Great Britain, with only one-fifteenth of the capital resources available to Great Britain. The funds available to Kenya for creating a new job are therefore 120 times (8 x 15) less than in Great Britain. So if Kenya had the luxury of creating the same type of jobs as Great Britain, it would have to pay 120 times as much for the privilege, relative to its income.[30]

Since this volume of capital is not available because of low internal savings and insufficient development funds, Kenya can create less than 1 percent of the jobs that Great Britain could create with a comparable capital structure. Many developing countries are faced with similar problems. Owing to lack of capital, they cannot exploit the opportunities that globalization has afforded the industrial part of the world, and hence cannot make any improvements in the employment structure in the long term.

Problems in the Labor Market

Since the end of World War II the global number of wage-earners has grown from 1.2 billion to 1.7 billion.[31] The International Labour Organisation (ILO) estimates that around 1 billion people are currently underemployed—that is, earning too little to satisfy their basic needs through their income. In many developing countries, up to 40 percent of the adult population is underemployed, and at the end of 1998 at least 150 million were completely without work.[32] Adequately paid jobs are a prerequisite for food security and quality of life, particularly for urban populations; for today's generation of parents, a reasonable income decisively influences the education of their children and hence the employment qualifications of the next generation. Current employment problems and associated losses in income play a major role in shaping future employment opportunities.

It is estimated that the number of employable persons will rise by 35–40 million a year until 2050. This increase means that by mid-century some 1.7–2 billion new jobs must be created even without making a dent in the present level of unemployment and underemployment. Even now, the difficulties of creating an adequate number of jobs under conditions of high population growth, with much lower capital intensity, are reflected in the dramatic scale of employment problems in practically all developing countries. Particularly in the poorest ones, these problems contribute to the vicious circle of poverty and population growth. Once more the gravest problems are found in sub-Saharan Africa, where 40 percent of the population lives in absolute poverty. Whereas only around 8 million people a year were reaching working age in the eighties, now the figure has more than doubled. Many find no work at all or have to accept a job that lies well below their skill level.

For ecological reasons alone (see the detailed description in the following chapter), job creation will be a major problem in the agricultural sector in most developing countries. If other sectors of the economy can no longer offer employment, this lays the foundation for a catastrophe with inestimable political and social ramifications. Historic population growth rates in countries like China or Algeria mean that more than twice as many people will be seeking employment over the next 50 years.[33] In many developing countries, demographically related employment problems are compounded by mass redundancies from formerly unproductive, staff-intensive state enterprises in the wake of economic reforms.

Over the past two decades, many developing countries have experienced an "educational revolution." Tragically, many young, well-qualified people are unable to find appropriate employment, and there is no sign of a parallel "employment revolution." On the contrary: the "lean production" mentality that evolved in industrial countries has also made inroads in many developing countries, creating an immense and highly explosive potential for social unrest that could further accelerate the downward spiral of poverty.

Intensification of Income Inequality

An early analysis by the World Bank documents a measurable correlation between population growth rates and the share of overall income held by the lower 40 percent of wage-earners. The higher the population growth, the lower the share of income in the lower brackets.[34] With a growing labor force entering a job market with limited absorbency, wages are being depressed. From a development policy standpoint, pressure on wage levels is undesirable, particularly in the lowest income brackets.

Since approaches to development policy are always colored by value judgments, opinion is also divided on how to evaluate any intensification of income inequality. Some development specialists see a positive side to the growing inequality of income distribution.[35] But 40 years of experience in development policy have not led to any concrete evidence in favor of widening income inequalities. In many countries the tendency has been more toward capital flight and conspicuous consumption by the wage-earning classes rather than toward reinvestment of profits and investment of savings in domestic labor-intensive facilities. Despite rapid economic growth in recent years, more than a billion people have had no opportunity to draw on this newfound affluence to at least meet their basic needs in a sustainable way.

Migration

Over the past few decades personal mobility has increased worldwide, and international migration is at a historic high. In addition to population shifts from rural to urban areas, more and more countries (primarily those suffering from the greatest population and environmental pressure) are experiencing streams of immigration and emigration. In the mid-nineties the total number of migrants was estimated to be at least 125 million, rising by 2–4 million a year.[36] More than half the world's migratory movements now occur between developing countries.

Migration is the result of a complex process dictated by a combination of factors. In some cases it is triggered by war, civil war, expulsion, or ethnic conflict and the associated violence and violation of human rights; in others, by a lack of employment and wage-earning opportunities; and in still others, by a deteriorating environment, lack of rain, or floods. The distinctions between, for example, "normal" migratory movements and refugee movements, legal and illegal or irregular migration, and conventional and mandatory refugees underlines the fact that migration is a heterogeneous issue.[37]

What is clear is that few of these migrants are motivated by mere wanderlust. Most are seeking better living conditions for themselves and their families. The incentive to migrate is most intense wherever the quality of life is perceived to be distinctly poorer than in the place of immigration. This motivation also explains the direction of some migration streams: if they can, many people leave Africa, Asia, and Eastern Europe for Western Europe, North America, and Australia or New Zealand. The exodus of relatively motivated and well-educated young people further lowers the standard of living in the country they abandon, particularly in rural areas. To some extent this negative effect can be offset if emigrants send money home once they have successfully settled and found lucrative employment, but this is rarely the case.

To solve migration problems, tailor-made programs must be developed and implemented that address all affected population groups. Needless to say, the most cost-effective solution is to prevent migration in the first place. This solution calls for development measures aimed first and foremost at promoting peace and improving the quality of life of people in regions prone to emigration. Since high birth rates also result in migration, social and population management measures must be initiated.

The prevention of migration can be seen as a legitimate motive for more con-centrated development assistance and promotion of reproductive health. Not only is it a worthier aim to improve the quality of life at home than to drive people to undergo the hardships and risks of migration; it is also more cost-effective.

Chapter 4

Pressures on Natural Systems

The doubling of the world population over the last 40 years has put enormous pressure on the natural systems that support all life on Earth. This chapter briefly describes the impact on water supplies, the quality and availability of arable land, the world's forests, and the biological diversity of the planet.

Fresh Water

Water is an irreplaceable raw material not only for every human being but also for every country's development. It is a basic prerequisite for the production of food. A sufficiency of water—through rain or artificial irrigation—produces a good harvest, while a lack of water endangers any chance of a harvest. Many industrial processes— in the chemical industry; in the production of paper, cement, glass, ceramics, steel, and iron; and above all in the production of energy—depend on an adequate supply of water. Finally, private households need clean water for drinking and cooking, for bodily and culinary hygiene, and for sanitary facilities. Moreover, water in sufficient quantity and quality is an essential element for many species on whose existence important ecosystems depend.[1]

How much water do we need? The regulating factors are supply and demand. Supply is dictated by a country's natural conditions and climate; demand is dependent on us, our practices, and habits. The supply of available water on Earth is not much more now than it was 2,000 years ago. Yet some 6 billion more people exist now than at the dawn of civilization, and all of them need water for agriculture, industry, and private consumption.

Many of these people are already suffering from water shortages. The global distribution of precipitation and—by extension—of river, lake, and underground fresh water resources is highly uneven between continents, countries, and even seasons of the year. Absolute water shortages pose major problems for many inhabitants of Africa, northern China, parts of India, Mexico, and the Middle East. More than 1 billion people in developing countries still have no access to clean drinking water; 2.4 billion lack access to sanitation facilities.[2] An international group of experts commissioned by the United Nations recently ranked water scarcity—defined as the existence of an available water supply of less than 1,000 cubic meters per person per year—as the second most urgent problem to be resolved by humankind, after population growth in regions with low resources.[3]

Wherever water is scarce, its quality deteriorates first, and eventually even the available quantity shrinks. Low-quality water has a devastating effect on human health: according to estimates by the World Health Organization, more than 5 million people die every year from illnesses caused by contaminated drinking water, lack of sanitation, and lack of water for hygiene. About half the inhabitants of developing countries are now affected by illnesses related to inadequate water stocks. A sufficient supply of clean water could reduce this illness and mortality rate by up to two thirds.[4]

Over the next 25 years world population is poised to grow by around 70–80 million annually. Naturally, these additional people will all need water. Since 20 percent of people in the poor regions of the world still have no access to clean water and almost 40 percent have no adequate sanitation, development strategies designed to meet the basic needs of this growing population will by themselves increase the requirement for water.[5] Added to this is a massive worldwide demand for water for other purposes. As world population trebled between 1900 and 1995, global water consumption rose sixfold—that is, twice as fast as population.[6]

Demand for water will continue to grow rapidly. Since 1970, global demand for water has grown by 2.4 percent a year.[7] Projections indicate that water withdrawals will increase by 35 percent between 1995 and 2020, reaching 5,060 billion cubic meters. Industrial countries are expected to withdraw 22 percent more water by then, with more than four fifths of that water going to industrial uses (see Figure 5). Developing countries are projected to increase their withdrawals by 43 percent in the same period and to experience a significant structural change in their demand for water. The share going to domestic and industrial uses is projected to double, to 27 percent, reducing the share available for agriculture.[8]

One of the primary pressures on water supplies is the need for irrigation. Since most of the land suitable for agriculture is already being cultivated, increases in food production must be achieved by raising yields by, among other things, increasing irrigated farming. According to Mark Rosegrant of the International Food Policy Research Institute (IFPRI), global consumption of irrigation water will increase by 4 percent by 2025, while that of non-irrigation water is expected to rise by 62 per-

Figure 5   Water Withdrawals for Various Uses, 1995 and 2020

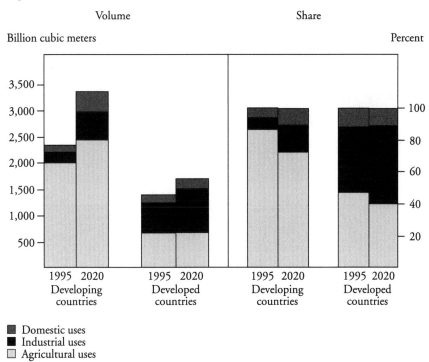

Source: M.W. Rosegrant, C. Ringler, and R.V. Gerpacio, "Water and Land Resources and Global Food Supply," paper prepared for the 23rd International Conference of Agricultural Economists, Sacramento, Calif., August 10–16, 1997.

cent.[9] Should this volume of water be unavailable, local food shortages may be unavoidable.

In the first half of the twentieth century, the acreage of land under irrigation doubled worldwide. Between 1950 and 1990 this feat was repeated.[10] Water consumption in the agricultural sector has risen by a factor of five since the fifties.[11] Around half the increase in food production achieved since the end of World War II is due to expansion of the artificially irrigated proportion of the world's arable land.[12] Were it not for this rapid spread of irrigated farming, the world would already be faced with major food supply problems.

Growth in irrigated area is projected to slow significantly. Worldwide, irrigated area is expected to grow at an average annual rate of 0.6 percent during 1995–2020, less than half the rate of 1.5 percent during 1982–93 (see Figure 6). In industrial countries, this area is projected to increase by only 3 million hectares, which is an

Figure 6   Irrigated Area in Major Regions, 1995 and 2020

Million hectares

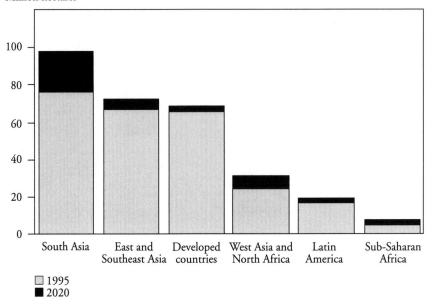

□ 1995
■ 2020

Source: M.W. Rosegrant, C. Ringler, and R.V. Gerpacio, "Water and Land Resources and Global Food Supply," paper prepared for the 23rd International Conference of Agricultural Economists, Sacramento, Calif., August 10–16, 1997.

average annual rate of 0.2 percent compared with 0.8 percent during 1982–93. And in developing countries, irrigated area is likely to increase by 37 million hectares by 2020, which is an annual rate of 0.7 percent—far below the rate of 1.7 percent during 1982–93.[13]

Although suitable arable land is a prerequisite for any agricultural operation, around 600 million hectares of potentially arable land suffer from a lack of water that inhibits production.[14] Without sufficient water, the arsenal of technical possibilities and hence the opportunities for higher yields and multiple cropping cannot be exploited. On average, irrigated farming is twice as productive as rainfed agriculture: almost 40 percent of all foodstuffs are grown on the irrigated 17 percent of the world's arable land. Data from the U.N. Food and Agriculture Organization (FAO) demonstrate the effectiveness of controlled irrigation for developing countries: it increases the per hectare yield of most food crops by 100 to 400 percent.[15]

Apart from increasing the volume of production, irrigated farming contributes to agricultural and rural development in other ways—for instance, by increasing the demand for labor and creating more employment opportunities in upstream and downstream sectors of the economy. Moreover, artificial irrigation allows farmers to switch to cash crops and hence improve their income. Irrigated farming now accounts for 80 percent of food production in Pakistan, 70 percent in China, and 50 percent in India and Indonesia; in Africa, only 10 percent of food is grown on irrigated land. FAO expects artificially irrigated land to be responsible for half or even as much as two thirds of future increases in crop yield. According to estimates by the World Bank and the United Nations Development Programme, it would be economically and technically feasible to irrigate an additional 110 million hectares of land. The resulting grain production could feed another 1.5–2 billion people.

Nevertheless, no matter how valuable irrigation technology is, we should not lose sight of its ecological and social drawbacks. First and foremost is the careless salinization of high-quality soil by proponents of irrigated farming in recent years. Irrigated farming also incurs social costs when, for instance, people are forced to resettle because dam construction projects destroy their habitats. Although such costs are significant, in the final analysis, the benefits of well-managed irrigation far outweigh its costs.

Without investment in irrigation, the prospects for an improved food supply are bleak for most developing countries. It may well be that efforts to increase irrigated farming in order to ensure food security will founder because of water scarcity. The amount of water required for this purpose would need to be trebled by 2025, but this volume of water will not be available for agriculture.[16] Since demand is also growing (and will continue to grow) in other consumer sectors—particularly the industrial sector and private urban households—the assumption even now is that agriculture will have to make do with far less water over the next 20 years. As a result, many countries will be forced to choose between agriculture and industry.

Distribution conflicts arise and intensify wherever natural resources become scarce. Even now, fresh water is the subject of national, regional, and international conflicts. As with most battles concerning the distribution of resources, the losers are characterized by poverty, rural life, and agricultural labor, whereas the winners enjoy relative affluence, urban lifestyles, and employment in sectors other than agriculture. The areas of concern in terms of water supplies are conflicts between rich and poor, between town and countryside, between present and future generations, and between different regions within a country as well as between different countries.

As with all complex global problems founded on a multitude of causes, water shortages cannot be resolved by a simple solution. Durable solutions to the problem of water scarcity must be regarded as a mosaic, where the overall picture has a large number of stones representing different areas of expertise and containing political, economic, and technical components. Population policy is an important stone in this mosaic, but not the only one.

Durable solutions must be found within national and international frameworks. There is a need for international cooperation and agreements governing the nonviolent resolution of water conflicts, for instance through providing funds for development cooperation. Promising, technically feasible approaches have already been found.[17]

A number of measures could help generate significant water savings if they were widely implemented:

- exploitation of all traditional methods of conserving rainfall (terracing, mulching, cistern construction);

- promotion of agricultural practices that conserve soil humidity (such as agroforestry and intercropping);

- increased protection of rainfed farming regions and the collection of flood and rainwater in basins that would subsequently be available for replenishing groundwater layers;

- improved farming methods: a study by the International Water Management Institute shows that even minor changes, for instance in rice farming, can result in water savings of up to 25 percent;[18]

- deceleration of deforestation and the promotion of reforestation on the banks of upper watercourses, in order to reduce the incidence of uncontrolled flooding and associated erosion and to increase soil capacity for water absorption;

- repairs to nonwatertight pipes in urban areas; and

- reduction of water pollution from industry and households and reprocessing of used water for irrigation.

The greatest loss of water occurs in agriculture. The effectiveness of irrigation is stagnating worldwide at the alarming rate of 40 percent. In other words, more than half of the water destined for crops never reaches them. The most promising means of saving water over the next few years is a marked improvement in irrigation techniques. China and India have advanced the furthest in spreading irrigation farming and could do a great deal to reduce the amount of water lost during the process by[19]

- reducing unused effluent,

- maximizing efficient use through better practices and technologies,

- controlling salinization and pollution,

- redistributing irrigation water from low-value to higher-value crops, and

- restricting access to a sustainable consumption level.

The consistent use of water-conserving technologies in agriculture, such as drip irrigation, could bring about quantum leaps in preserving water resources. Over the past 20 years, Israeli farmers using drip irrigation methods with an effectiveness level of up to 95 percent have managed to double their food production without increasing water consumption. While the use of drip irrigation has grown by a factor of 28 since 1970, the "market share" of this type of irrigation is still less than 1 percent.[20] Many developing countries would gain direct and cost-effective benefits from the transfer of this technology.[21] For crops where root irrigation via plastic tubing is not economically viable, low-pressure drip irrigation systems could bring about water savings of 20–30 percent.

The major gap between supply and demand must be addressed by building institutional capacities and institutions charged with managing this scarcity, and by improving information systems.

Counterproductive water subsidies must be discontinued. As Mark Rosegrant has noted: "Most of the world does not treat water as the scarce resource that it is. Both urban and rural water users receive massive subsidies on water use; irrigation water is essentially unpriced; in urban areas the price of water does not cover the cost of delivery."[22] When people have no financial incentive to save water, they tend to squander it. Prices that reflect the ecological value of water, particularly for urban areas and their resident consumers, are thus an important instrument for controlling demand.[23] Graded, progressive tariffs must be introduced to safeguard against unreasonable entrance thresholds for poor households and rural smallholders: low charges for basic consumption, rising gradually for consumption beyond this level.[24]

In addition, there is need for improvement in global, regional, and national databases to ensure timely recognition of the rising demand for water and to safeguard against potential failures and shortages. Water must be incorporated into an integrated development and land-planning concept, and preference must be given to small-scale solutions.[25]

Finally, concerted political consensus campaigns must be waged in regions scarce in water resources. An optimum method of sharing water must be found where it is scarce, and conflicts must be largely avoided. National water policy reforms to ensure the most efficient use of water can help defuse tensions over shared supplies. Preventive management of water conflicts affords the opportunity of leveraging important pools of knowledge and expertise.[26] Nonviolent solutions to conflict are always cheaper and more durable.

Intergovernmental efforts along these lines have had mixed success to date:

A 1977 agreement between India and Bangladesh allocated 63 percent of the dry season flow of the Ganges at the India/Bangladesh border to Bangladesh. However, the agreement has not been in effect since 1988, and water disputes remain a serious source of conflict. More significant headway has been made on talks between Jordan and Israel over the Jordan and Yarmuk Rivers and on shared groundwater resources. However, the lack of participation of Lebanon and Syria in these talks has made it difficult to reach comprehensive settlement on the use of water from the Jordan and Yarmuk Rivers.[27]

Water consumption levels cannot possibly drop to a tolerable level for at least 10 years. This is because, first, we can only be moved to change our habits and ways of thinking with great difficulty, and second, the planning and implementation of water projects takes time. Since there is a risk that tension over precious water resources will turn into armed conflict, it is in the interest of all those affected by current or potential water deficiency and the global community to act swiftly and cooperatively. The successful resolution of water scarcity calls for a wide range of economic, agricultural, social, and technical measures. In every case, success will also require measures to slow population growth, because finite water resources and unlimited population growth are irreconcilable.

Soil Erosion and Quality

What is true of the decline in water supplies and its consequences for human development applies in like measure to soil. When a country or region has to accommodate more people because of population growth or migration, the pressure on all available resources—including arable land—increases accordingly. Nowhere is the statement "a limited planet cannot accommodate an unlimited number of people" more apt than when applied to the finite availability of fertile soil.

Like water and air, earth is an irreplaceable element essential to human life and the functioning of ecosystems. People need land to cultivate food crops; over 90 percent of all human and animal foods are produced on the land. What is more, we exploit land for our habitat, our workplace, and many other purposes. Not just any "land mass" will do for the cultivation of food: we depend on "fertile soil." Since degraded soil can take centuries to regenerate, fertile soil must be viewed as a non-renewable resource.

Approximately 1.5 billion hectares of arable land are available for food production. Around half of this is in developing countries, where more than 80 percent of the world lives. Over the past three centuries world population has grown by a factor of eight while the area of agricultural land has grown only by a factor of five.[28] The consequences are staggering. In 1960 there were still 0.44 hectares of arable land per person in the world. By 1999 this had dropped to a mere 0.22 hectares, and by the middle of the twenty-first century the figure will sink to 0.15 hectares.[29] More than half of world population growth is occurring in countries that even now have practically exhausted their potentially arable land.

Although studies indicate that soil quality has been relatively stable on 75 percent of the world's agricultural land since 1950, degradation is widespread and accelerating on the other 25 percent.[30] Sara Scherr of the University of Maryland notes that productivity "has declined substantially on approximately 16 percent of agricultural land in developing countries, especially on cropland in Africa and Central America, pasture in Africa, and forests in Central America. Almost 75 percent of Central America's agricultural land has been seriously degraded, as has 20 percent of Africa's and 11 percent of Asia's."[31]

Between 5 million and 12 million hectares of arable land are destroyed each year by salinization, erosion due to flooding, or overexploitation.[32] If land continues to be lost at the current rate, an additional 150–360 million hectares will be forced out of production by 2020.[33] Another 20 million hectares suffer loss of productivity.[34] In the eighties, FAO was already expressing concern that approximately 544 million hectares—18 percent of the world's arable land—would be irreversibly lost if no corrective measures were taken to preserve them.[35] To date little action has been taken.

Water- and wind-induced erosion—the loss of topsoil and its organic components—is endangering 29 percent of food production in rainfed farming lands. Soil erosion through water is one of the most severe problems in the tropics, in many areas on a scale that cannot be corrected through natural soil regeneration. India, for instance, is losing 16.35 tons of soil substance per hectare a year, but only 4.5–11.2 tons can be regenerated by appropriate management.[36] Water erosion along riverbanks is particularly damaging, since the best soils are being carried off just where access to a source of irrigation is easiest.[37]

The interplay between various factors such as climate, topography, soil quality, and vegetation cover dictates the degree of natural erosion. Human intervention exacerbates erosion, since it generally disrupts soil-stabilizing vegetation. Wind-induced erosion has the gravest consequences in arid and semiarid regions where, for instance, soil is stripped by overgrazing of its vegetation cover. Over 22 percent of land in Africa north of the equator and 35 percent in the Near East suffers from wind erosion. Under extreme conditions, a hectare of land can be stripped of 150 tons of earth within an hour.[38]

Erosion is a problem in many different areas. Population pressure in some regions leads to the farming of land that is not suited for cultivation (steeply sloped, for instance). Deforestation and the removal of hedges and bushes expose soil to wind and water and affect its capacity for regeneration over the long term. All these processes lead to major loss of productivity. They impede the ability of soil to absorb water and hence prevent flooding. The indirect, environmental impact of erosion on neighboring states downstream can sometimes be far greater than the direct damage. Since earth mass transported downstream by rivers fills up other waters downstream, flooding at this juncture is even greater and more devastating. The pictures that have reached us from Bangladesh in recent years illustrate what may soon be a commonplace event.

For many years the agricultural lands of Earth have suffered from soil degradation, to the extent that now 38 percent of all soil used for agricultural cultivation is damaged. As soil quality deteriorates, yield per hectare also declines. This decline threatens food security either directly in the form of lower food intake, or indirectly in the form of reduced purchasing power due to fewer opportunities to market harvested products. Case studies in West Africa showed a measurable correlation between the mortality of children under five and the extent of soil degradation.[39] Soil degradation has played a role in most contemporary famine crises.[40]

The role it could play in the future is described by Scherr:

> Future soil degradation is likely to have its greatest impact on agricultural incomes as yields decrease and input costs grow in irrigated, high-quality rainfed, and densely populated, lower-quality lands. Countries or subregions that depend upon agriculture as the engine of economic growth will probably suffer the most. Degradation will threaten the consumption of poor farmers above all. The greatest problems will probably occur in the densely populated marginal lands of sub-Saharan Africa and Asia, especially where markets are less developed and industrial inputs expensive.[41]

Of course, the problem of soil degradation has been recognized for decades.[42] Various sources indicate that more than 2 billion hectares of land have irreversibly lost their productivity during the past thousand years.[43] Now, however, the pace of degradation appears to be accelerating. An analysis by Russian authors concluded that since the beginnings of agriculture 10,000 years ago, Earth has been losing humus at the rate of around 25.3 million tons a year.[44] Over the past 300 years, this accelerated to approximately 300 million tons a year, and to 760 million tons a year in the last 50 years. According to Rozanov, Targulian, and Orlov, more soil has been irreversibly lost in the past 10,000 years than is presently farmed.

More than 83 percent of soil degradation is attributable primarily to wind and water erosion. While no comprehensive information is currently available on the effects of climate change on soil in developing countries, the intensification of weather phenomena such as El Niño and the increased incidence of extreme storms is expected to result in an acceleration of the process of soil degradation.[45] In places like Bangladesh, where floods occur as a result of global warming and the associated rise in sea level, large sections of arable land will literally disappear.

Desertification is a particularly pressing problem that endangers the food security of 250 million and possibly as many as 850 million people. In the eighties, B. Messerli and colleagues estimated the annual production loss in areas affected by desertification at approximately $26 billion—equivalent to almost half the amount currently spent on development work.[46] Desertification occurs wherever traditional, soil-conserving farming practices have been abandoned as a result of increasing population pressure. Needless to say, inappropriate agricultural policies, failure to address the needs of small farmers, inadequate resource management, and other factors have also contributed to the present state of affairs in certain countries.

Soil deterioration and destruction should not be regarded as irreversible or even unavoidable. There is a wide range of agricultural, ecological, land entitlement, and other measures that can stop or even reverse soil degradation.[47] Negative trends can be halted and even reversed through adaptation to changed conditions, as well as through innovation and technical progress. Soil degradation is the result of not only the large number of people who practice agriculture but also their farming methods and the place where they practice them.[48] Appropriate preventive measures and solutions have been around for some time.[49] Once more, the failure to solve current problems lies not in the lack of knowledge but in deficiencies in implementing this knowledge.

Sustainable solutions, however, are not simple to translate into practice. Scherr describes the important role that government could play:

> A necessary though not sufficient step in combating soil degradation is to implement policies that support broad-based agricultural development and enhance farmers' incentives and capacity for land-improving investment. Many soil degradation problems could then "self-correct" to a considerable extent by 2020. In some areas, a policy environment that promotes information dissemination about already existing good land husbandry practices and supports research on technologies to reduce conservation costs may be sufficient for addressing degradation concerns. But

policies and investments targeted to specific development pathways, farming systems, soil types, and degrees of degradation are also necessary.[50]

The deterioration of soil quality is a slowly encroaching process that is practically invisible over the years.[51] Once the lack of organic material and other deficits impede production potential so severely that fertilizer no longer helps, the soil is irreversibly damaged. Thus the first decisive step must be to create an awareness of the problem. Better education and easier access to information for farmers would help them identify the causes and urgency of the problem early.

This creates the foundations for corrective action in the form of alternative farming methods (such as crop rotation, cultivation of other crops, ploughing depth, and use of fertilizers), conservation measures (terracing; the planting of trees and hedges; construction of reservoirs to collect surface water; or use of compost, mulch, or ground covers), or other solutions.

Often, it is also essential to introduce land tenure reforms and other economic incentives, particularly for small farmers. Poorly defined property rights or common grounds only encourage maximum exploitation and discourage soil maintenance practices.[52] This deficiency is also to blame for the ecologically destructive practice of shifting cultivation. Soil in secure-tenure lands is generally better cared for and can regenerate wherever possible. While land reform is not sufficient on its own, it is often a necessary precondition for a changed attitude to earth and soil. Land reforms will only become a successful element in development policy when small-scale farmers obtain the advice they need, coupled with credit programs and accompanying measures implemented on a case-to-case basis.

State intervention on a participatory basis and supported by incentives, coupled with investments in soil-conserving infrastructures, enhances the quality of land management and helps keep soil degradation within manageable limits. Such measures should be implemented wherever the private cost of degradation prevention (including labor force and opportunity costs) is higher for farmers than the direct benefits for their yields, and especially where the private cost is higher than the social benefits.

Farmers have an interest in conserving the foundations of their existence. They will react by adopting new techniques if these offer a net benefit and if they have access to suitable technical tools.[53] If dire necessity precludes any possibility of addressing their own interests or society's future interests, help must come from elsewhere in the form of state or development aid. Successful land management covers an entire catalogue of economic, agricultural, social, and technical measures. The same is true for soil degradation: simple, single-cause solutions provide no answer to problems that have many causes, and measures to slow down population growth are once more important.

Forest Degradation

Like the world's water resources and fertile lands, forests perform essential ecological, social, economic, and cultural functions. They are among the world's most diverse, widespread, and least-understood ecosystems. Tropical rain forests are not only important from an aesthetic and philosophical standpoint; they are also valuable for a wide range of other reasons.

Forests form the basis of the timber industry and enable the production of a wide array of consumer durables such as bamboo, rattan, and rubber. Over and above this, forests offer an abundance of fruits, spices, mushrooms, nuts, berries, herbs, honey, and other foodstuffs. Plants indigenous to the rain forest and of major importance to the global economy include cocoa, bananas, citrus fruits, coconuts, and sugarcane.[54] Consequently, forests create jobs and income for indigenous peoples and provide recreational and cultural space.

Forests play an important role in stabilizing the water level and preventing erosion. Hence they make a significant contribution to ensuring the basis for agricultural production. Added to this, they are an important source of freshwater. Nowhere else are the life forms of flora and fauna so diverse, the variety of species so vast, and hence the genetic pool so large as in tropical forests. The more we learn about the genetic makeup of Earth's life forms, the more biodiversity gains in importance.

Finally, forests function as a global "air conditioning system," balancing out temperature and thus regulating regional climates; they influence the hydrological cycle and precipitation volumes through evaporation and transpiration; and, most important from a global perspective, they absorb damaging greenhouse gases and are believed to be an important "carbon sink." The negotiations on the climate change treaty since 1997 have emphasized the key role of forests in mitigating global climate change.

The world's forests, particularly its tropical rain forests, are of immeasurable importance to sustainable national, regional, and global development. Their products alone are worth several hundred billion dollars.[55] But in terms of regional and global environment, the services derived from forests are priceless.

In 1995, the forested surface of Earth covered an estimated 3.45 billion hectares—roughly one quarter of its overall surface.[56] Of this, 56 percent was situated in developing countries. Tropical rain forests currently account for about half of the world's rain forests and almost one sixth of all deciduous forests. "Forest plantations" account for some 3 percent of global forest cover.

The threat to the world's forests is nothing new. It was documented some 20 years ago in a report to Jimmy Carter entitled *The Global 2000 Report to the President.*[57] This well-researched warning went largely unnoticed, and the destruction has continued unabated since then. The losses have been most notable in tropical regions.

Almost half the forests that once covered Earth have now disappeared. Between 1980 and 1995, the world's forests declined by another 180 million hectares.

Many people in industrial countries decry the state of tropical forests but overlook the fact that the forests on their own doorsteps also require urgent attention. Two thirds of Europe's forest cover has disappeared, and less than 1 percent of old forest there remains.[58]

The exact extent of forest degradation is difficult to ascertain. The Consultative Group on International Agricultural Research estimates the rate of tropical forest degradation during the mid-nineties at 29 hectares per minute; according to this calculation, the extent of forest loss between 1980 and 1990 is equivalent to the combined territory of Ecuador and Peru.

Tropical forests are being destroyed for many reasons.[59] The reasons behind the damage differ from one country to another, and the speed of forest destruction is indexed to the prevailing social, economic, and political framework—such as development support for small-scale farmers, the importance of agriculture for employment and national revenues, and land reform issues.

Unquestionably, however, the key factors underlying accelerated forest degradation are as follows:[60]

- slash-and-burn, primarily or exclusively for subsistence production;

- agro-industrial land use for commercial crops (such as coffee or palm oil) or fodder (soy, for example, or maize);

- extensive livestock farming, primarily cattle;

- harvesting of firewood;

- felling of timber for commercial purposes (tropical wood has particularly attractive properties and is relatively cheap compared with its substitutes); and

- clearance for mineral resources or electricity generation (dams).

According to estimates by the United Nations Population Fund, 79 percent of tropical forest cover destruction can be attributed to increased population pressure and the associated need to extend agricultural surface areas for small-scale shifting cultivation, firewood, and commercial timber harvesting.[61]

The consequences of forest degradation include soil erosion, firewood scarcity, and the degradation of the habitats and cultures of indigenous peoples. In addition, tropical rain forests play an important role in regulating regional climates as well as the global climate. They provide atmospheric balance by producing enormous quantities of oxygen and consuming huge volumes of carbon dioxide during the photosynthesis process. The destruction of tropical forests would result in the release of large quantities of harmful substances, which in turn would change the chemical composition of Earth's atmosphere.

The decline in tropical forests acting as "greenhouse gas storage tanks" is responsible for 20–30 percent of carbon emissions, 38–42 percent of methane emissions, and 25–30 percent of nitrogen dioxide emissions.[62] The potential effect of these greenhouse gases on climate change is known.[63] The destruction of forests through deforestation as well as the burning of biomass is changing the microclimate, and the reciprocal mechanisms of trace gases between atmosphere and biosphere—the emission and reduction of climate-relevant gases (such as nitrogen oxide and carbon dioxide)—are undergoing dramatic change.

In conclusion, the benefits of forests still tend to be drastically undervalued. They are regarded as spacious uninhabited regions that acquire economic significance only when they begin to be exploited for forestry or agriculture.[64] Unless political commitment to the protection of the forest is stepped up, and unless all the agreed resolutions are implemented in industrial and developing countries, there is no hope of reversing the trend.[65]

The situation urgently calls for more detailed and interdisciplinary research on the broad spectrum of benefits of forests and the scale of their degradation, as well as the immediate application of currently known practices of integrated and sustainable forestry. North-South cooperation through, for example, development aid and technology transfers is essential for humankind as a whole.

Loss of Biodiversity

Probably the most dramatic result of uncontrolled deforestation is the decline in biodiversity.[66] Biodiversity covers a wide range of organizational levels of life: first, there is genetic diversity within a species, then species diversity, and so on up to and including ecosystem diversity (different types of landscape and habitat).[67] The term is so broad that it could also be taken to cover the diversity of all manifestations of life, even human, cultural, and ethnic diversity.[68]

Biodiversity entails inestimable potential material benefits. Forests contain an invaluable supply of genes, and they house useful insects for combating agricultural pests in other regions. The import of a single beneficial insect from the Cameroon enabled Malaysia to increase the value of its palm oil production by $150 million a year.[69] Crossbreeding of wild relatives (for wheat, maize, or potato farming) is of enormous importance to world nutrition, for example, in the fight against plant disease or for research into yield security. Tropical diversity is a key factor in assuring food security for indigenous peoples.

Since tropical forests are currently being destroyed faster than any other habitats on Earth, the scale of species extinction is larger than at any previous time in human history. It is estimated that one species per hour has been dying out since the mid-eighties.[70] Of the 45,000–50,000 species of plant in tropical Asia alone, 300 a year disappear forever. The implications for humankind are incalculable. We cannot even quantify the consequences of the extinction of a single species, since little is known about the complex interrelationship between different plants and animals—the web of life.

Most people acknowledge the risk to large, attractive animals like the Siberian tiger, the mountain gorilla, and the humpback whale—known as the charismatic megavertebrates. And emotions can be mobilized through public campaigns to save them from extinction. Yet the loss of 95 percent of species goes largely unnoticed. If the current trend toward destruction of the biosphere continues, it is feared that 10–50 percent of all species will die out within the next 50 years.[71]

Species diversity is of intrinsic value. It is part of the creation that is only on loan to us and the integrity of which we are duty-bound to maintain. The destruction of tropical forests is by no means the only cause of species diversity loss. All the fish reserves of the world's seas are now on the threshold of overuse or are already used up. In this century alone, almost 1,000 species of fish have been threatened with extinction through overfishing.

Other tropical habitats at risk include coral reefs, whose biological diversity is justifiably compared to that of tropical rain forests; mangroves; island fauna; and alpine-tropical biomes.[72]

While loss of biodiversity may be difficult to quantify, it remains an indisputable fact. The chain of underlying causes includes population growth and the resultant destruction of or change in fragile ecosystems, whether in the form of deforestation, the draining of wetlands to create new cropland, or the spread of urbanization and settlement accompanied by infrastructure. Further links will be added to this chain in the future—the greenhouse effect and the depletion of the ozone layer, which directly affect biological diversity. Yet the main link in this causal chain remains the spread of humankind to previously untouched regions.[73]

Assuring Food Security
for a Growing Population

Enough food is available today, if equally distributed, to meet the basic needs of each and every person in the world. Yet in this world of plenty, more than 800 million people—almost one eighth of humanity—are food-insecure. More than 160 million preschool children in the developing world—one out of every three—are malnourished or severely underweight for their age.

The burden of assuring food security for all the world's people is great and becoming greater. Over the next 50 years world population is set to increase by 3 billion, and possibly by as much as 4.5 billion. To meet the market demand of a growing and urbanizing population, most experts believe cereal production needs to be increased by about 35 percent and meat production by over 55 percent in the next 20 years.[1] Food production would need to increase even more to meet the physical food needs of all people, even those who cannot afford to buy food in the marketplace. Yet the resources needed to feed this population are dwindling, since freshwater is becoming scarce, agricultural land is losing fertility and becoming scarce, and forests are disappearing.

As past experience shows, producing enough food on a global level is not enough to ensure food security for the world's people. As much as possible, it is vital that local food production meet local food demand. In developing countries, agriculture is not only a supplier of food, but also the main source of employment. Meeting the food needs of developing countries on an ongoing basis with surpluses from industrial countries is not logistically feasible. And most developing countries do not have enough foreign exchange available to meet most of their food needs through imports. Finally, the sound practice of agriculture can be a tool for sustaining the landscape and protecting the environment in developing countries.

Defining Food Insecurity

Food security is defined, in its most basic form, as access to the food required for a healthy life by all people at all times. Achieving food security has three dimensions: enough high-quality food must be available, households and individuals must have access to this food, and people must be able to make use of this nourishment with the help of clean water, adequate sanitation, and health care.

This definition of food security includes not only food, which provides carbohydrates, fats, and proteins for energy as well as vitamins and minerals, but also clean drinking water. Clean water is an important factor in health as well as for physical and mental performance. In hot climates and under hard physical labor, the need for water intake far exceeds the daily minimum requirement of two liters.

There is general agreement nowadays that the energy requirement of a healthy adult who performs light work is approximately 2,400 kilocalories (kcal) a day. People doing more physical labor require up to 4,000 kcal. The minimum energy for people in developing countries would be 1,500–1,800 calories, according to the U.N. Food and Agriculture Organization (FAO). Any intake below this level has a negative impact on health, increases the risk of illness, and impedes mental and physical activity. In children, it slows down the rate of growth, inhibiting physical and mental development. The body becomes increasingly weak, ultimately dying, in the worst case.

In theory, nutritionists distinguish two types of household food insecurity—chronic and transitory—but in reality these two types are closely intertwined. Chronic food insecurity is a persistently inadequate diet caused by the continual inability of households to acquire needed food by either buying it or producing it themselves. This all-too-common problem is rooted in poverty. Transitory food insecurity, on the other hand, is a temporary decline in a household's access to needed food due to factors such as instability in food prices, production, or incomes.[2] In its worst form, transitory food insecurity can result in famine. Typically, the chronically food-insecure are hardest hit by transitory food-insecurity problems.

Food insecurity can look different in rural areas than it does in cities. In urban areas, food security depends primarily on wages relative to food prices and on the level of employment. Further, the miserable health environment in poor urban areas sometimes makes the urban food security situation qualitatively different. Typically, calorie consumption is lower in urban areas than in rural areas, partly because of differences in activity levels. And although the prevalence of food insecurity is lower in urban areas, urban poverty with chronic food insecurity will become an increasingly important problem in the future as the world continues to become more urban.

Food insecurity is more than caloric inadequacy. Micronutrient deficiencies also remain widespread. About 2 billion people suffer from iron-deficient anemia, more than 2 billion are at risk of iodine-deficient disorders, and 180 million people are vitamin A deficient.[3] Relatively little attention has been paid to other important micronutrients such as zinc, riboflavin, and calcium, and the extent of global deficiencies in these remain unknown. The consequences of micronutrient malnutrition include higher mortality and morbidity, lower cognitive ability and work production, impaired reproduction, and forgone economic growth.

There are strong links between poor diets and infectious diseases. A person's nutritional condition influences his or her susceptibility to illness and dictates the course of the disease. Poorly nourished people, especially children, are much more likely than the well-nourished to die from infection. Because of this reciprocity between infectious diseases and dietary deficiency, reliable statistics on food-related deaths are difficult to obtain. The number of people who actually starve is probably "low," but only compared with the number who die as a result of the indirect effects of chronic malnutrition.

Causes of Food Insecurity

Unavailability of Food

In a world increasingly integrated through trade and political-economic ties among nations, sufficient global availability of food is of growing importance for household food security. So far, the world has kept up with the challenge of population growth. But global food availability cannot be taken for granted in the long run in view of continued population growth, increased land scarcity, and difficulties in achieving sustainable increases in yields of food crops. And availability of food at the household level requires that food be available not just globally or nationally, but in local or community markets, which in turn requires relatively smooth market operations, functioning infrastructure, and a free flow of information.

National, regional, or local availability of food is determined primarily by food production, stockholding, and trade at any of these levels. Variations in any of these can contribute to food insecurity. For instance, increased variability of cereal production has been shown to increase the variability of food consumption significantly.[4] Recent evidence indicates that year-to-year variability in world food production may be increasing.[5] Fluctuations in a country's capacity to import food (which is a function of export earnings, world prices, and debt-service obligations, among other variables) also contribute to food insecurity by affecting the local availability of food.

Seasonal variations in production and seasonally high food prices are often important contributors to transitory food insecurity of poor households, which can escalate over time into chronic food insecurity and malnutrition.[6] Sudden changes in incomes and prices affect the ability of households to obtain food that is available. An important source of fluctuations in seasonal food prices lies in the costs of storage and failure to manage public food stocks adequately. Further, the ability of households to demand adequate food effectively is governed by outside events (such as price shocks, war, or deteriorating terms of trade), domestic policy changes, and random weather-induced events such as droughts, interacting with existing technology and a given resource endowment.

Poverty

Poverty is a complex and multidimensional social phenomenon. It consists not only of the lack of essential criteria for material affluence, but also of the absence of opportunities and choices that are of key importance to human development: a long, healthy, creative life; a reasonable standard of living; and freedom, self-worth, self-respect, and the esteem of others.[7] In 1999 the World Bank estimated that 1 billion people were living in "absolute poverty" in developing countries. Absolute poverty—defined as a daily income of $1 or less—is a state of "degrading living conditions" (according to then World Bank President Robert McNamara, in his visionary Nairobi speech in September 1973) and is characterized by disease, illiteracy, undernourishment, and neglect to such an extent that the prerequisites for a decent life no longer exist.[8] And the number of people obliged to live on less than $2 a day is about 3 billion—half the world in 1999.[9]

Nowadays we know the microeconomic, macroeconomic, social, and ecological factors that lead to poverty.[10] As with other development issues, however, the concrete causes of poverty vary by region, household, or household member. Individual conditions of poverty can be traced to an array of factors that vary according to social structure, ethnic origin, religion, and culture. It has long been acknowledged that poverty particularly affects women.[11]

People who are too poor to provide for themselves using their available productive resources, who have to survive on an insufficient income, are condemned to hunger—even if food is in plentiful supply elsewhere in their society. According to Amartya Sen, hunger is usually (but not exclusively) based on the quantity of food generated. His analysis and proposals revolve around the concept of "entitlement": the right to goods, services, or privileges through work, capital, normative rights (the solidarity of the community or protection by traditional security systems), and food assistance.[12] As a 10-year-old he experienced the great Bengal famine of 1943, when 2–4 million people died of starvation despite sufficient food supplies. The cause, as with the great Irish famine of 1846–50 and the great Ethiopian famine of 1973, was the export of food from the famine region to the more lucrative markets of the cities. As a result, people literally starved when full granaries were within reach.

Causes of Famine

The human race has repeatedly been afflicted by famine and famine-related death, even in Europe. The Irish potato blight of 1846–50, which resulted in the deaths of 2–3 million people, is one of the best-known European famines. Yet it is by no means the only one. In the mid-eighteenth century almost 5 percent of the population of France died from famine. Moreover, devastating famines resulting in millions of deaths affected Russia between 1920 and 1921 and the Ukraine, where 5 million or perhaps even 10 million people died between 1930 and 1932.[13]

People will not soon forget the shocking pictures broadcast into our living rooms at the end of the Biafra war (late sixties), during the drought in the Sahel zone (mid-seventies), and during civil wars in Ethiopia (mid-seventies and eighties) and the Sudan (at present): emaciated wrecks with wasted arms and legs, swollen stomachs, and enormous, staring eyes. The cause of these human catastrophes was a drastic reduction in the food supply, and in some cases a complete lack of food for weeks on end, resulting in the death of tens of thousands of people. There are also many other examples:

- In China, 10 million died between 1876 and 1880; in 1920–21, 4 million starved to death; and the devastating famine of 1959–61, which the government kept secret, claimed 30 million victims.[14]

- In West Bengal in 1943, 2–4 million people died.

- In 1992, tens of thousands of people in Somalia suffered when food supplies dried up in the wake of the civil war.[15]

- Also as a result of civil war, tens of thousands starved in 1995 and 1996 in Rwanda, Burundi, and Liberia, and very recently in the Sudan.

The risk of famine is still current and real. In the mid-nineties, conflicts and their aftermath put 80 million people at risk of hunger.[16] According to a March 2001 FAO report, 33 countries around the world are facing exceptional food emergencies.[17] Civil strife and population displacement are responsible for the crisis in half of these countries, including Russia (Chechnya), Afghanistan, southern Sudan, Angola, Congo, and Sierra Leone. A close relationship exists between conflict and declining per capita food production; during the period 1970–93, countries experiencing conflict in sub-Saharan Africa produced about 12 percent less food per person in war years than in peacetime.[18] Inhumane policies still kill more children than do lack of rainfall or other climatic extremes.[19]

In a 1998 study of famine in Africa, Joachim von Braun, Tesfaye Teklu, and Patrick Webb drew three principal conclusions about famine at the turn of the twenty-first century:

First, present-day famines in Africa are largely the result of military conflicts that arise due to oppressive, unaccountable, and nonparticipatory government. There is no doubt that little progress can be made in famine relief, and even less in prevention, while conflict continues to drain human and capital resources.

Second, famine in Africa is inseparable from chronic poverty and risk. Although famine characteristics differ between countries, the underlying poverty conditions that contribute to famine in Africa are quite similar: lack of employment opportunities; limited household assets; isolation from major markets; low levels of farm technology; constraints to improvement in human capital; and poor health and sanitation environments. Although factors such as political and military conflict and drought contribute to famine, they do so mainly where people are vulnerable in the first place, and where resilience to external shocks has already worn thin.

Third, famines do not happen suddenly. They are an accumulation of events and policies that progressively erode the capacity of countries as well as households to deal with short-term shocks to the economy and food supply. These shocks often take the form of environmental extremes, but the conditions that promote household vulnerability to such extremes develop over long periods. Misguided macroeconomic and trade policies have been part of the problem in most famine-prone countries, and conditions established by past policy failures cannot be rectified in the short run.[20]

Consequences of Food Insecurity

Food security and adequate nutrition are beneficial outcomes in themselves as well as important inputs to economic development. Food is essential to survival, and people are more emotionally secure and better off psychologically when they have food security. Food insecurity and the frequently extreme efforts made by affected households to avert it lead to much human suffering.

Improved adult nutrition leads to higher farm productivity and higher productivity in the labor market. High levels of morbidity, due in part to insufficient nutrient intake, can reduce work time directly as well as indirectly through the need to take care of sick family members. They can also divert household resources away from farm or nonfarm investments and toward medical care.

Poor nutrition and health impair cognitive development and school perform-ance, with consequent losses in productivity during adulthood. Poor nutrition and health in early childhood can have long-term consequences that affect a child's later progress in school. Among school-age children, nutritional deficiencies are respon-sible in part for poor school enrollment, absenteeism, early dropping out, and poor classroom performance. Educators have often overlooked the significant improvements in school performance that can result from nutrition and health interventions.[21]

Not only does food insecurity have deleterious effects on households and indi-viduals, but the effort to achieve food security may also exact a heavy toll on house-holds if, for example, it involves people spending most of their income on obtaining food, leaving little for other basic necessities of life such as housing and health. House-holds may achieve temporary food security at the cost of losing substantial assets and incurring future debt, thus digging themselves deeper into the mire of poverty. In the extreme case, a household that uses almost all its resources to achieve food security in the present renders itself highly vulnerable to food insecurity in the future.

The efforts of food-insecure households to acquire food may also have impor-tant implications for the environment and the use of natural resources. Many poor and food-insecure households live in ecologically vulnerable areas,[22] and inappro-priate or desperate land use practices can cause environmental degradation that can further undermine their livelihood. Food-insecure households do not deliberately degrade their resource base without any thought of the consequences; on the con-trary, they are fully aware that their food security is at stake if their environment is threatened. The food-insecure and the poor often have to choose between short-term satisfaction of food needs and long-term environmental conservation.

The search for food security may also have important implications for a region's demographic situation, especially if it leads to short- or long-term migration to other areas in search of employment and income or, in some cases, in search of relief food. This migration can result in an increased number of female-headed house-holds, a higher dependency ratio in the sending areas,[23] and changes in the dynam-ics of the labor market. The receiving areas, mostly urban slums, experience considerable food-security strain from the influx of migrants.

Who and Where Are the Food-Insecure?

As we consider how to feed billions more people in the coming decades, it is impor-tant to take stock of how far we must go to achieve food security for Earth's

Figure 7   Distribution of the World's Food-Insecure People, 1995–97

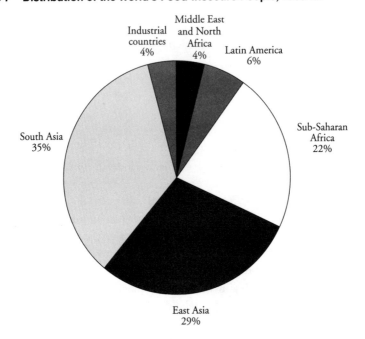

Source: FAO, *The State of Food Insecurity in the World 1999 and 2000* (Rome: 1999 and 2000).

current inhabitants. The location and identity of today's food-insecure may suggest areas of greatest risk for the future.

An estimated 824 million people worldwide are food-insecure. Of these, 34 million (less than 5 percent) live in industrial countries (see Figure 7). The remaining 790 million live in the developing world, almost half of them in just two countries—India and China. The number of food-insecure people in these two nations, 368 million, is equivalent to the population of Canada, Mexico, and the United States combined. While the absolute number of food-insecure people is largest in South and East Asia, the proportion of the total population that is food-insecure is highest in sub-Saharan Africa. Every third person there gets too little food for a healthy, productive life (see Figure 8).

Some progress has been made in changing this situation. The number of food-insecure people in the developing world dropped from 960 million in 1969–71 to 790 million in 1995–97. Although a decline of 170 million over a quarter-century might appear small, the developing world's population increased from 2.6 billion to 4.6 billion over this same period. A more appropriate measure, therefore, would be the proportion of the total population that is food-insecure. By this measure, progress has been impressive—the share of food-insecure has been cut in half, from

Figure 8   Food-Insecure People as a Share of Total Population, 1995–97

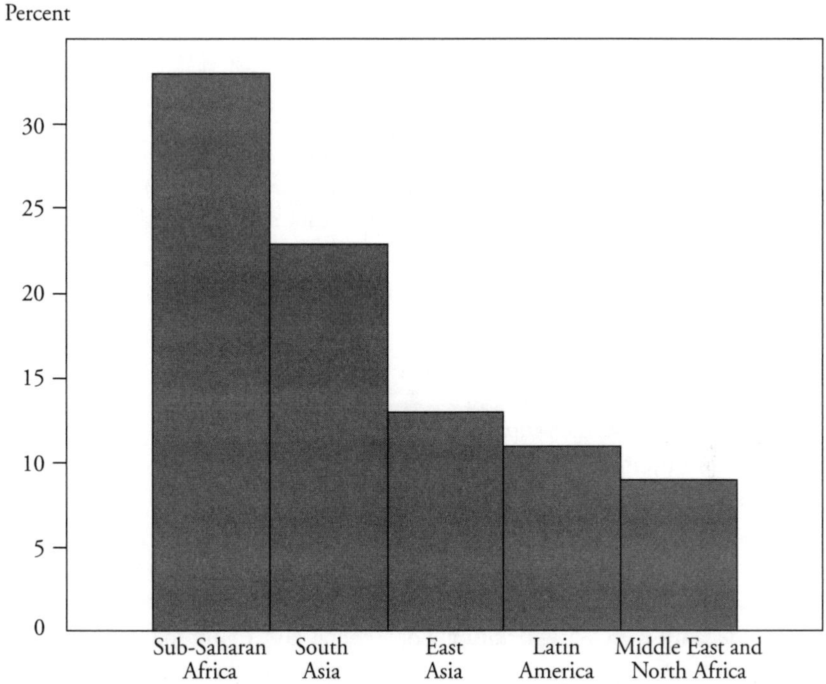

Percent

Source: FAO, *The State of Food Insecurity in the World 1999 and 2000* (Rome: 1999 and 2000).

37 to 18 percent, during this time. Similarly, there has been some headway made in reducing child malnutrition, with the number of afflicted children dropping from 204 million (47 percent of children) in 1970 to 166 million (31 percent) in 1997.

Yet progress in the developing world is uneven. While the number of food-insecure people declined by a staggering 260 million in East Asia between 1969–71 and 1995–97, it remained virtually unchanged in South Asia and Latin America and dropped only slightly in the Middle East and North Africa. And sub-Saharan Africa has emerged as a new locus of hunger, with the number of food-insecure doubling in this period to reach 180 million.

Depending on factors such as agroecological characteristics, access to land, diversity of income sources, and state of development of the economy, food-insecure households can be members of different socioeconomic and demographic groups in different areas. Nevertheless, some common characteristics of food-insecure people are clear—and poverty is a central one. A recent comparative study looked at incomes of malnourished rural poor people in 13 survey areas in Africa, Asia, and Latin America and found a number of common sociodemographic characteristics:[24]

- Food-insecure households tend to be larger and to have a higher number of dependents and a younger age composition.

- Ownership of land or access to even small pieces of land for farming has a substantial effect on the food-security status of rural households, regardless of income level; the prevalence of food insecurity tends to be higher among landless or quasi-landless households, who are much more dependent on riskier sources of income than farm income and on the diversification of the rural economy.

- Women's income has an important influence on the food-security status of the household, and female-controlled income is more likely than male-controlled income to be spent on food and nutrition.[25]

Typically, food-insecure people either spend a large share of their income on staple food consumption or allocate a large share of their production resources to subsistence food production in normal years, or both; yet they may barely meet their needed levels of dietary intake.

The available evidence suggests that most of the rural poor in developing countries live in what are known as less-favored areas. The areas that fall into this category include lands with low agricultural potential because of limited and uncertain rainfall, poor soils, steep slopes, or other biophysical constraints, as well as lands with high agricultural potential but limited access to infrastructure and markets, low population density, or other socioeconomic constraints. Cereal yields of less than 1 ton per hectare are common in less-favored areas, which often suffer from deforestation, overgrazing, soil erosion, and soil nutrient depletion.[26]

Different types of risks affect different groups of food-insecure households and their members in different ways. The most severe problems arise from simultaneous combinations of common risks. For example, children in poor smallholder households that have limited income diversification may be affected if their families experience a bad crop or loss of employment and are located in an area of civil unrest. The possible combinations are numerous. To improve household food security, the specific risks need to be identified so that effective and efficient risk-reducing actions can be developed.

Agriculture's Track Record and the Special Case of Sub-Saharan Africa

Just looking at global food production, it would appear that all our problems should be solved. Over the past 30 years food production has risen steadily, even doubling—a historic record.[27] These remarkable production figures are based on a relatively minor expansion of agricultural lands as well as a significant increase in yields per hectare. The latter was the decisive factor that led to an almost fivefold increase in grain production during the twentieth century.

Most of these successes were achieved in industrial countries. Whereas an American farmer at the beginning of the twentieth century was producing enough food to feed 7 people, an American farmer now can feed 96 people.[28] This achievement was due to

- the use of new seed types, resulting in higher per hectare yields and multiple harvests;

- a significant increase in the use of fertilizers;

- a doubling of artificially irrigated croplands;

- the protection of food cultures against blight, weeds, and pests; and

- the use of efficient machinery.

Global data such as these and the doubling of food production over the past 30 years tell only part of the story, however. They are "unreal" averages that aggregate the very high production figures of a few countries with the extremely poor results of others. In many industrial countries farming has been discontinued on some arable lands due to fears of a sustained drop in prices, with the result that production has been deliberately reduced. Available technological components are by no means universally deployed. In most countries in sub-Saharan Africa, political mistakes, neglect of subsistence farmers, deficiencies in agrarian policy, shortcomings in agricultural extension services, and other factors have conspired to produce a steady decline in per capita food production.

There are a host of underlying causes for Africa's susceptibility to famine crises. Theoreticians on the left of the ideological spectrum believe that Africa has been damned to underdevelopment by a combination of imperialism, colonialism, and capitalism.[29] They are right insofar as there is little dispute that 400 years of exploitation by Europeans provided a poor springboard to self-sufficient development. Theoreticians on the right and center-right lay the blame elsewhere, citing underdeveloped capitalism and the resultant lack of economic growth that, if present, would eventually generate widespread affluence—an argument they support with some illuminating examples.[30] Others blame the African condition on the lack of "dynamic impulses and opportunities in African culture and in particular in African value systems and social class structure" or on the imposition of unsuitable nation-state structures.[31]

Yet others content themselves with the bald statement that the people of sub-Saharan Africa are simply "too lazy" and are therefore themselves to blame for their crises. A diplomatic formulation of this argument has been presented by John Kenneth Galbraith.[32] Against such accusations of indolence it must be noted that almost no other people in the world work harder or longer than African women. Not only are they responsible for cultivating 80 percent of the food on their continent; in addition to performing the vast catalogue of household and child-care duties regarded by their men as "women's work," they also devote hours to other hard physical tasks (collecting firewood, fetching water, weeding, and so on). These women rarely enjoy commensurate rights despite their heavy workload. According to Ugandan President Yoweri Museveni, their husbands would do well to draw more on their own energy reserves. (Museveni claimed that the male employees of state institutions stop working long before exhaustion sets in.)[33]

In contrast to these specious arguments, an analysis by the International Food Policy Research Institute (IFPRI) suggests the following factors as a plausible explanation for the persistence of food insecurity in sub-Saharan Africa:[34]

- the negative impact of the cold war on agricultural and land development policy;

- chronic unrest, war, and civil war and the crises induced by such conflicts;

- mismanagement of national resources by political leaders; and

- the inability to build local institutional capacities in critical areas.

Wherever malnutrition is endemic, the main culprit tends to be ill-conceived government policies that discriminate against small-scale farmers. Problems related to infrastructure, capital supply, and marketing often give rise to an unsuccessful pricing policy. High population growth over the years has been accompanied by a shrinking of agricultural land area and the quantity of available water. Sub-Saharan Africa will continue to be forced to rely on food assistance.

If, in order to account for changes in eating habits, "cereal cropland" rather than "agricultural land" is used as a yardstick, the scarcities become even more apparent. According to Worldwatch Institute, cereal cropland per person has shrunk globally from 0.23 to 0.11 hectares since 1950.[35] For individual countries with high population growth, the situation will deteriorate drastically over the next few years.

Figure 9   Population and Food Production Indexes for Sub-Saharan Africa, 1961–2020

Index: 1961 = 100

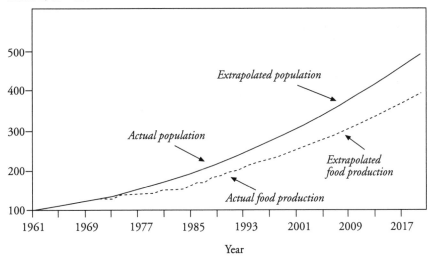

Source: Data for 1961–66: Food and Agriculture Organization of the United Nations, FAOSTAT database, <http://faostat.fao.org> (accessed August and September 1997); extrapolations for 1997–2020: authors' estimates.

Between now and 2050 it is predicted that Nigeria's cereal cropland will drop from 0.15 to 0.07 hectares per person. In Pakistan the figure is expected to shrink from 0.08 to 0.03 hectares per person—the size of a tennis court—over the next 50 years. These predictions herald a precarious situation, since all these processes exacerbate poverty and impede food production.

The population growth rate in sub-Saharan Africa has exceeded the rate of growth in food production since the early seventies, and the gap is widening, resulting in declining per capita food production. Simple extrapolations of the trends in population and food production growth since 1961 show a further increase in the gap between population and food production (see Figure 9). This is exactly the gap predicted 200 years ago by Thomas Malthus. Several recent developments, however, suggest that Malthus's shadow over sub-Saharan Africa could finally be waning.

First, Malthus's predictions grossly underestimated the potential of productivity-increasing technology. Where such technology has been effectively developed and used, such as in Asia, food production has expanded much faster than population. In sub-Saharan Africa, the potential of appropriate productivity-increasing technology has yet to be realized. Maize yields for Africa and Asia were virtually the same in 1961, but since then they have tripled in Asia and quintupled in China while they have remained stagnant at around 1 ton per hectare in Africa.[36] Yet there are encouraging signs that productivity-increasing technology is beginning to accelerate yield growth of African food crops. For example, the introduction of improved maize varieties has resulted in productivity increases in West and Central Africa at rates as high as 4 percent a year during 1983–92.[37] Some counties experienced particularly high rates of growth in maize production during this period, including Burkina Faso (17.1 percent), Ghana (8.3 percent), and Mali (7.5 percent), albeit starting from low levels.

If Malthus is to be proved wrong in sub-Saharan Africa, a much greater effort must be made to ensure that farmers have access to appropriate production technologies and that policies are conducive to expanded productivity in staple food crops. In addition to new initiatives and expanded support for agricultural development, more must also be done to reduce population growth. Sub-Saharan Africa's annual population growth rate is projected to decline between 1993 and 2020. Yet the number of people added to the region each year is expected to increase until at least 2020, a consequence of past high rates of population increase. Moreover, this region's projected annual population growth rate of 2.33 percent during 2015–20 will be more than twice the growth rates in other regions.[38] Population growth of this magnitude will severely constrain efforts to increase income and improve welfare, while at the same time greatly increasing the need for food.

Prospects for Assuring Food Security

Researchers at IFPRI have constructed a model showing the world's likely food situation in the year 2020 under various scenarios. This model, the International Model for Policy Analysis of Commodities and Trade (IMPACT), uses the United Nations' medium projection of population growth for its most likely scenario.[39] Under this scenario, global demand for cereals will increase by 35 percent between 1997 and 2020, reaching 2.5 billion tons; demand for meat will increase by 57 percent, reaching 327 million tons; and demand for roots and tubers will increase by 39 percent, reaching 901 million tons. These large increases in food demand will result not only from population growth but also from urbanization, income growth, and associated changes in lifestyles and food preferences.

Almost all the increase in demand will take place in developing countries (see Figure 10). These will account for about 85 percent of the 654-million-ton increase in the global demand for cereals between 1997 and 2020. Surprisingly, they will account for a similarly large share of the 119-million-ton increase in demand for meat products. China alone is forecast to account for one quarter of the global increase in demand for cereals and for two fifths of the demand for meat. (Although

Figure 10   Total Demand for Cereals and Meat Products, 1997 and 2020

Million metric tons

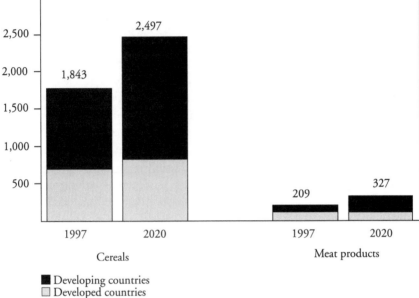

■ Developing countries
□ Developed countries

Source: M.W. Rosegrant, M.S. Paisner, S. Meijer, J. Witcover, *2020 Global Food Outlook: Trends, Alternatives, and Choices*, Food Policy Report (Washington, DC: IFPRI, 2001).

India's population is projected to increase much faster than China's between 1997 and 2020, its share of the global increase in demand for cereals is expected to be about half that of China's while its share of the increased demand for meat is expected to be only one tenth that of China.) By 2020, developing countries as a group are forecast to demand twice the quantity of cereals and meat products as industrial countries.

At the same time, however, a developing-country person in 2020 will consume less than half the quantity of cereals as someone in an industrial country and slightly more than one third of the meat products. Per capita demand for cereals and meat products in developing countries will continue to lag far behind that in other nations, although the gap will begin to narrow in the case of meat. The disparities in demand can be explained by low incomes and greater dependence on roots and tubers for sustenance.

Nevertheless, a demand-driven "livestock revolution" is under way in the developing world, with profound implications for global agriculture, health, livelihoods, and the environment. Between the early seventies and the mid-nineties, the volume of meat consumed in developing countries grew almost three times as much as it did in industrial ones.[40] With continued population growth, urbanization, income growth, and changes in lifestyles and food preferences, meat demand in the developing world is likely to double between 1997 and 2020, to 213 million tons, and to increase by 16 percent in industrial countries, to 114 million tons.

While increased consumption of livestock among high-income people in industrial countries who regularly consume excess calories could lead to health problems, including cardiovascular diseases, increased consumption of even relatively small amounts of meat and milk among low-income people in developing countries could improve their nutritional status by supplying necessary proteins and micronutrients as well as calories. Similarly, although rapidly increasing livestock production can cause serious damage to the environment, it can be harmonious with the environment when appropriate types and levels of production are in place.

In response to the strong demand for meat products, developing countries' demand for feedgrain is projected to almost double between 1997 and 2020, to 435 million tons, while demand for cereals for direct human consumption is projected to increase by 40 percent, to 1.04 billion tons.

The world's farmers will have to produce 35 percent more grain in 2020, most of which will have to come from yield increases. IMPACT projections suggest that farmland cultivated with cereals will increase by only 6.6 percent, or 46 million hectares, by 2020, with much of the growth concentrated in fields with the relatively low-yielding cereals of sub-Saharan Africa. A modest expansion in cereal area is forecast for Latin America, but virtually no growth is projected for Asia or industrial countries. Increases in cereal area in the developing world are expected to contribute only 15 percent of the cereal production needed to meet demand between 1997 and 2020. Therefore, improvements in crop yields will be required to bring about the necessary production increases.

Yet growth in farmers' cereal yields is slowing. In both industrial and developing countries, the rate of increase in cereal yields has slowed since the heyday of the Green Revolution of the seventies. This is due partly to reduced use of inputs like fertilizer, reflecting low and falling cereal prices, and partly to low levels of investment in agricultural research and technology. Poorly functioning markets and lack of appropriate infrastructure and credit are also contributing factors. Without substantial and sustained additional investment in agricultural research and associated factors, it will become more and more difficult to maintain, let alone increase, cereal yields in the longer term. The gap in average cereal yields between industrial and developing countries is slowly beginning to narrow, but it is widening considerably within the developing world as sub-Saharan Africa lags further and further behind other regions, particularly East Asia.

Figure 11   Number of Food-Insecure People, 1969–71, 1996–98, 2015, and 2030

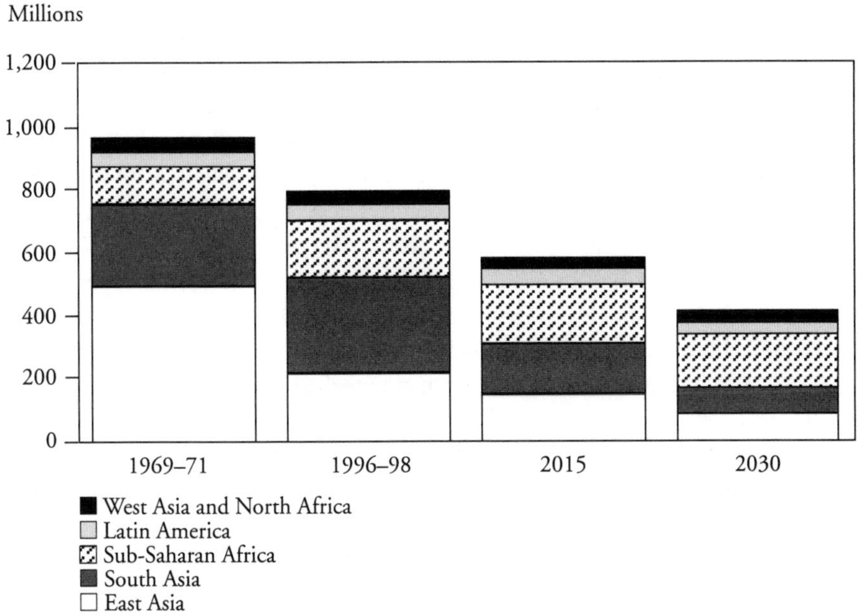

Millions

West Asia and North Africa
Latin America
Sub-Saharan Africa
South Asia
East Asia

Sources: FAO, *Assessment of the World Food Security Situation,* prepared for the Committee on World Food Security, 27th Session, Rome, May 23–June 1, 2001; FAO, *Agriculture Towards 2015/30,* Technical Interim Report (Rome 2000).

Despite large increases, cereal production in the developing world will not keep pace with demand. Net cereal imports by developing countries will almost double to fill the gap. IMPACT projections suggest that the developing world's net cereal imports will increase by over 90 percent between 1997 and 2020, reaching 202 million tons. About 12 percent of the developing world's cereal demand is projected to be met through net imports from the industrial world, up from 9 percent in 1997.

With the exception of Latin America, all major regions are forecast to increase their net cereal imports. A massive increase for South Asia, from 3 million tons in 1997 to 21 million tons in 2020, is expected because domestic production in the region is not projected to keep up with income and population growth. In Pakistan, problems with salinity and waterlogging in the main cereal production areas will limit crop yield growth, while population growth will be rapid. Sub-Saharan Africa's net cereal imports are expected to remain low relative to its needs because of lack of foreign exchange and entrenched poverty.

Projections of food production and consumption to the year 2020 offer some signs of progress, but prospects for a food-secure world remain bleak if the global community continues with business as usual (see Figure 11). Already FAO has noted that the recent World Food Summit goal of halving the number of food-insecure people from 800 million in 1995 to 400 million by 2015 will not be achieved until 2030 at the earliest.

IMPACT projections suggest that there will be similarly slow progress in reducing child malnutrition. Under the most likely or baseline scenario, 132 million children under the age of six—one out of every four children—will be malnourished in 2020. This represents a decline of only 20 percent from 166 million in 1997. Hence, one out of every four children in developing countries will still be malnourished in 2020, down from one in three earlier. South Asia and sub-Saharan Africa are expected to remain hot spots of hunger and child malnutrition. Despite improvements, South Asia is forecast to be home to a third of the developing world's malnourished children in 2020. Sub-Saharan Africa is the only region projected to experience an increase in the number of malnourished children between now and 2020, by 6 million or 18 percent.

IMPACT projects that under an optimistic scenario the number of malnourished children in 2020 could drop to 94 million. Elements of an optimistic scenario include increases in projected income growth in developing countries, increases in crop yield growth in both industrial and developing countries, increases in cultivated area and irrigated area in developing countries, improvement in social indicators, and low-variant population projections. Conversely, the number of malnourished children could climb to 175 million in 2020 under a pessimistic scenario, in which case all the elements just mentioned tend in the opposite direction. Hence the policy choices made and investment decisions taken, or not taken, will profoundly influence how many and who will be food-insecure in the future.

Policies for Food Security

Policy efforts to assure enough food for a growing world population must recognize that food security involves not only food production, but also access; not only technologies, but also policies and institutions; not only national food availability, but also household availability; not only rural areas, but also cities; and not only food quantity, but also quality.

Agricultural growth has a central role to play in improving the availability of food and enhancing access. Many of the world's poor and food-insecure are rural-based and, even when not engaged in their own agricultural activities, they rely on nonfarm employment and income that depend in one way or another on agriculture. Moreover, agricultural growth is a catalyst for broad-based economic growth and development, particularly in low-income countries: agriculture's linkages to the nonfarm economy generate considerable employment, income, and growth in the rest of the economy. Very few countries have experienced rapid economic growth without agricultural growth either previously or simultaneously.

Developing countries can make a number of public investments that will greatly facilitate agricultural and rural growth. Areas of investment include

- appropriate use of modern technology, including biotechnology and information and communications technologies, for the benefit of the food-insecure and the poor, through yield-increasing crop varieties and improved livestock as well as through yield-increasing and environmentally friendly production technology;

- reliable, timely, and reasonably priced access to appropriate inputs such as tools, water, and plant nutrients;

- an integrated nutrient management approach that seeks to both increase agricultural production and safeguard the environment for future generations;

- strong extension services and technical assistance to effectively bridge the gap between researchers and farmers;

- improved appropriate infrastructure, particularly in rural areas;

- efficient, effective, and low-cost markets, especially for agricultural inputs and outputs, while assuring access to productive resources by the poor to enable them to compete on equal terms; and

- creation and expansion of small-scale credit and savings institutions that are available to small farmers, traders, transporters, and processing enterprises.[41]

These investments need to be supported by an enabling policy environment. This includes trade, macroeconomic, and sectoral policies that do not discriminate against agriculture, and policies that provide appropriate incentives for the sustainable management of natural resources.

As already noted, availability of food is a necessary but not sufficient condition for food security. Therefore policies to reduce child malnutrition and improve food security should include the following:

- investing in improving women's education and status;

- fighting hidden hunger or micronutrient deficiencies through fortification, supplementation, diversified diets or changed eating habits, and the breeding of nutrients into staple crops through conventional methods or biotechnology;

- tackling urban food insecurity by improving urban livelihoods, supporting environmentally sound urban agriculture, promoting healthy physical environments and adequate caring and feeding practices, and designing more participatory urban programs and strategies; and

- effectively addressing prevalent and emerging health risks and diseases.[42]

Special attention must be paid to sub-Saharan Africa and South Asia. Sub-Saharan Africa is the only region where the number of malnourished children has consistently increased since 1970 and the only region where it is projected to continue increasing through 2020. South Asia is home to half of the world's hungry and malnourished. Together, sub-Saharan Africa and South Asia are the new locus of hunger in the developing world.

Conclusion

Projections of the global food outlook in the coming decades make starkly clear the scale of the task ahead. The greater the world's population, the greater the task of feeding it. A food-secure world will require that decisionmakers across the globe show more concerted political will and pursue more sound investments in agricultural and overall economic development as well as in population control than they have to date. After all, even today astonishing advances in agricultural productivity and human ingenuity have not yet translated into a world free of hunger and malnutrition.

With increased political complacency or greater-than-anticipated deterioration of key variables such as water availability, land quality, human resource development, and technological innovations, the mixed outlook for the world food situation could be significantly worse. Ideally, projections of the sort given here will serve as a wake-up call and contribute to productive policy change. Then, the test of a successful projection will be its failure to come true,[43] for ultimately, our behavior, priorities, and policies will determine the nature of the world food situation in the twenty-first century.

Chapter 6

Population and Sociocultural Norms in Traditional Societies

E very society has social, religious, and cultural norms that influence birth rates.[1] These norms also had an effect in pre-modern Europe.[2] Cultural norms that currently limit birth rates in developing countries include sexual taboos (for example, refraining from intercourse during breastfeeding), lengthy postpartum abstinence (many cultures separate young mothers from their husbands for three to five months), prohibition of remarriage for widows (in India, for one), a taboo on pregnancy for women whose children already have their own children, and so on.[3] Cultural factors also determine the length of time for breastfeeding, thus influencing the duration of natural infertility.

But there are also many factors that strongly support fertility, including social factors such as early marriage or specific religious and cultural rules.[4] When societies do not differ greatly in terms of income, education, or the social and material conditions of life, cultural factors—religion, caste, or type of family—usually become important determinants of human reproductive behavior.[5] In some religions, a high number of children is still considered to be a sign of divine favor.[6] For example, Muslim societies in northern Africa and the Middle East have higher birth rates than countries with similar economic and social conditions.[7]

These issues call for careful reflection. Religious affiliation should be considered in relation to the local context: for example, birth rates in Indonesia have been decreasing for many years.[8] Women there have more rights and better educational opportunities than women in other Muslim countries such as Pakistan or in states where women are heavily discriminated against and birth rates remain high.[9] When religion sanctions high birth rates at the same time society assigns a low status to women, the synergies that arise have dramatic demographic consequences.

The Status and Roles of Men and Women

Although women have experienced important progress in terms of social status, health, and educational opportunities in recent decades, the world today is still largely dominated by men. Apart from many other disadvantages in terms of social development, this also has negative demographic impacts: archaic proof of manhood consists in the number of children a man begets. Women are considered merely the biological means to this end. Thus societies characterized by patriarchal systems or other forms of male dominance, as well as by gender-related division of roles, have higher birth rates than societies where gender relations are based on equality.[10] Family planning is also less accepted in male-dominated societies.[11]

In the social system of traditional societies, gender roles are firmly fixed. The extended family is far from just an entity in which several generations share housing and living space. It is above all an extremely complex system of reciprocal duties in which it is difficult to distinguish economic components from social components. Most extended families have a strictly patriarchal structure. This means that the order of dominance and influence, as well as social relations and resources, are determined and controlled by the oldest men in the family.[12] Patriarchal systems are usually closely linked with traditional rural modes of life and labor that are determined by a council of male elders. The greater the number of family members in a traditional household, the more favorable the conditions for a division of labor, and the less the need to employ paid laborers.

In such societies, networks of family ties strengthen the individual's social safety net and may allow a family to have greater political power within the village or the tribe. In most cases, these networks also have positive economic consequences.[13] There are only two ways of broadening this network of relationships—and thus of increasing one's political and economic influence: by having many children and by arranging their strategically favorable marriages.

The absolute decisionmaking power of patriarchs in economic matters has an impact on the number of children conceived that is not always obvious and immediate, but nevertheless effective. Why do adults, generally sons, accept their fathers' decisions? Here, too, the reasons are primarily economic: they hope to benefit through submission, or they fear losing a great deal through opposition.

Social pressure also has a great influence. If a pregnancy does not follow soon after a marriage, husbands must endure gossip about their possible impotence, while wives must endure rumors about their infertility; the quality of the marriage or the husband's power over his wife may also be questioned. The absence of a pregnancy can also trigger a patriarch's displeasure, since he too may be exposed to suspicions of weakness, thus endangering his social status. Tragically, unwanted infertility (through illness, for example) can have serious negative consequences for women.

In patriarchal societies, infertility is often considered so great a personal failure that it can lead to contempt, persecution, and even divorce.[14]

According to J.C. Caldwell, birth rates in developing countries will only start to decline when traditional production units are replaced by more modern forms of organization, giving family members the opportunity to make autonomous decisions about their lives.[15] When demographic change occurred in Europe, the dissolution of the extended family was considerably accelerated because income was available outside the family, higher education was widely accessible, and the influence of certain cultural factors was declining. The incredible speed of industrial development led to a collapse of cottage industries, since the goods that used to be made in the family could now be produced at far lower cost through mass production. The growth of egalitarian political systems also had an impact on behavior within the family.

Still, gender relations continue to have an impact on all aspects of life in societies throughout the world.[16] They influence decisions about how the food and nutrition needs of the family are met, who goes to which school, what roles people play in society, the amount of power and authority they have, and the kinds of income they have access to. Discrimination against women exists in every part of the world. It affects the quality of their jobs and their wages, the length and quality of their training, their access to health care services, and so on.

Conditions are particularly inequitable for women in developing countries that have patriarchal structures. Relationships between men and women in these countries are characterized by a lack of partnership and by extreme forms of discrimination; domestic violence against women is not uncommon.[17] In patriarchal extended families, relations between spouses are not necessarily any better than those that a husband might have with his brothers or his father and uncles. The role of a woman, her status as an individual, her opportunities for development, and her position with regard to men in the same society are roughly comparable to the position of the lowest classes in feudal societies.[18]

Lack of equality in gender relations always has undesirable consequences for the quality of life of women and girls. In the context of social preference for sons, the consequences can even be deadly: wherever this preference is found in South Asia, the mortality rate among girls aged 2 to 5 is higher than among boys, contrary to the global biological trend. The United Nations Population Fund considers this to be the result of boys' receiving more positive attention than girls—they are better nourished and receive medical treatment more rapidly when ill, as well as being generally better cared for.[19] Even if female infanticide perhaps still plays only a small role, its existence proves the severity of the problem.[20]

In numerous East Asian countries where the preference for sons is highly developed, gender relations have changed notably in favor of young boys—not least of all thanks to selective abortion after prenatal determination of a fetus's sex. Although it is difficult to make exact statistical measurements, at least 60 million girls—and perhaps even as many as 100 million—are estimated to be "missing" in some Asian countries.

Wherever women are socially disadvantaged because of their sex, wherever they are deprived of appropriate education and training, and wherever patriarchal systems make them economically and socially dependent and confine them in a social environment where their duties have no just relation to their rights, fundamental ethical norms are violated. This in itself would be reason enough to advocate change. But there is yet another reason for social change that benefits women: wherever women are oppressed, birth rates are high and remain high; wherever women are autonomous, birth rates decrease.[21] The reasons for this are fairly easy to understand.

When governmental assistance (such as the education of girls), mass information campaigns (social marketing, for instance), or modern attitudes promote gender equality and equal partnerships between men and women, women have a greater degree of social and economic freedom. Under such conditions, there is a greater likelihood that women will have an income-generating occupation outside the home and thus contribute to their family's livelihood. Moreover, if girls receive a better education, they have better chances of finding a job in a modern economic sector; when this happens, they have greater opportunities for professional development and for planning their lives so that their role as mothers is one of many roles. Wherever this happens, the importance of women within the family increases, giving women more opportunities to influence matters of concern to the whole family. If women had their way in the world, the global population growth rate today would be 20 percent lower.

Men and Family Planning

In many traditional societies in developing countries, anything concerning children is a woman's responsibility. This fact explains why women were (and still are) the main target group of programs advocating family planning and reproductive health. But in every developing country with a traditional culture, men are the decision makers: they determine sexual behavior, they decide about the use of contraceptives, and they practice—or choose not to practice—"safe sex." Men control all household resources, including women. Women's availability, their mobility, and their time are in the hands of men.[22]

For this reason it is not very sensible and efficient for family planning and reproductive health programs to focus only on women. The fact that the "male factor" has been given too little if any consideration in the past is probably one of the main reasons that many family planning programs have not succeeded as well as they could have. Gender-specific role models create an unbalanced distribution of power between partners: in proportion to the duties they are assigned, women are given far too few rights. Paradoxically, preventing unintended pregnancies is a woman's responsibility, although women do not have the right to decide whether they will have children or not.

Because it is a sensitive topic in political and cultural terms, sexuality is usually excluded from discussion—although it is a topic with obvious relevance to family planning and reproductive health programs. It is also a complex issue, but this complexity dissolves as soon as the sexual realities faced by women are considered in an unprejudiced way. The efficiency of programs and their capacity to offer services and information that actually promote responsible parenthood and reproductive health depend on such knowledge.

Work concerned with HIV/AIDS has shown how important it is to address the issue of sexuality and to involve men in the discussions.[23] Women are particularly exposed in this respect because they are not in a social or cultural position to impose a change of male sexual behavior. Since the International Conference on Population and Development in Cairo, there is at last a growing awareness that programs that aim to change sexual and reproductive behavior cannot have a sustainable and broad impact if they only focus on women.

Women's Right to Education

Ample evidence shows that education and training influence a society's birth rate.[24] This is even more obvious with regard to the educational level of women (see Table 4).[25] Education for women is three times as effective in decreasing the birth rate as education for men.[26] A comparison of 98 developing countries showed that secondary school education for women was the central factor in lowering the birth rate.[27] Other studies have arrived at similar conclusions.[28] The main reason is that longer school attendance increases the age at which girls marry and have their first pregnancy.[29] Other studies reveal that women who have a better education wish to have fewer children because they have the possibility of leading more autonomous lives; they are also in a better position to fulfill this wish.[30]

Totally apart from demographic considerations, adequate education and professional training—including further career training—are key requirements for development and the fulfillment of human rights. Education and training are among the fundamental prerequisites for self-development, social security, and equal participation in the economic, political, and cultural life of any society. Education is a necessary component in successful promotion of greater justice, liberty, and tolerance.

Table 4   Number of Children per Mother According to Mother's Level of Education, Selected Countries, 1993–2000

Country	Average number of children of mothers with:		
	No education	Primary school	Secondary and higher education
Bolivia (1993–94)	5.8	5.6	3.1
Burkina Faso (1998–99)	6.2	4.7	2.3
Côte d'Ivoire (1998–99)	6.2	4.7	2.3
Egypt (1994)	4.7	3.7	2.9
Ethiopia (2000)	6.2	5.1	3.1
Indonesia (1994)	3.1	3.1	2.5

Source: Demographic and Health Survey reports and *Comparative Studies; Macro International, Fertility Levels, Trends, and Differentials* (Calverton, MD: 1998).

Yet a large share of women in many developing countries are still being denied the fundamental human right of education and the acquisition of knowledge. This in turn diminishes their chances to be something other than mothers and wives. The situation is particularly deplorable in patriarchal societies, where the dominant opinion is that education is largely unnecessary for girls and will be of no use in their future lives. In countries where girls must fulfill traditional duties and become members of their husbands' extended families when they marry, schooling is indeed superfluous—if not a likely "cause of rebelliousness." The attractiveness of educated wives for "modern-minded" sons of patriarchs who "accept" them lies largely in the ability of these women to increase the family's material prosperity and social prestige. Women on the "marriage market" in the upper classes are a case in point.[31]

According to *The World's Women*, a report first presented by the United Nations in 1991,[32]

- women in the developing world attend school only half as long as men,

- the number of illiterate women increased worldwide by more than 50 million in the previous 20 years (half of the women living in rural areas in developing countries still cannot read and write today), and

- the situation is just as bad in the informal educational sector and in the professional training sector: although women can make major contributions to economic development, they benefit from only a tiny share of available educational resources.

Women's education also helps significantly lower infant and child mortality rates as well as birth rates. A mother's level of education determines the extent to which children will benefit from goods and services that have vital nutritional, hygienic, and sanitary functions. Improved infant and food hygiene, better nourishment in infancy (through breastfeeding), the age at which children switch to adult food, and an elementary knowledge of medical facts create synergies that lead to a considerable and rapid decrease in infant and child mortality rates.[33]

One study of reductions in child malnutrition in developing countries from 1970 to 1995 found that improvements in women's education were responsible for 43 percent of the reductions—by far the most important factor.[34] Although improvements in women's status overall accounted for only 12 percent of the reductions, this in combination with the education factor contributed to more than half of the drop in the prevalence of malnutrition in developing countries during this period.[35] As the authors note:

> Education of women is a powerful weapon against malnutrition: increased knowledge and skills enable women to earn higher incomes, and thus enhance household food security, and education improves the quality of day-to-day care women give to their children. Women's status relative to men's influences children's nutritional status through its effects on the mental and physical condition of the women themselves and through women's autonomy and ability to influence how household resources are allocated.[36]

A mother's level of education and knowledge is also the decisive factor when it comes to accepting and using existing institutions that promote the health of mother and child. Mothers will have their children vaccinated only if they know about the physiological causes of diseases and do not lay the blame for an illness on some supernatural phenomenon (punishment for sins, for instance, or evil spirits or offended ancestors). They will use oral rehydration therapy only if they are convinced that it can help save their children from dying of diarrhea. Finally, they will adequately and regularly check the weight of their babies only if they are aware that this is of decisive significance to their children's well-being.

Mothers who learn skills crucial to their children's well-being are also the first to recognize how positive these skills are. They are open to further ideas and are motivated to modify their behavior in other ways—with respect to family planning, for example. They are aware that they have the power to improve the quality of their own and their children's lives.

Political and Economic Rights for Women

Although women have the right to vote in virtually every country and constitute more than half of the voting population, they are underrepresented in parliaments and only rarely have leading public roles. Consequently, they have few opportunities to contribute to shaping the national and communal policies that could improve their lives or help them make such improvements.

Even in industrial countries, women occupy only 12–14 percent of the highest public positions. Moreover, these are usually in areas categorized as typically "female"—education, culture, and issues related to women or children. Men have the more powerful positions: in business, finance, and national defense. In most developing countries, the situation is even more precarious: women have only 6–9 percent of the leading public positions. In public administration and private companies, most women have subordinate roles. The higher the position and the corresponding salary and the greater the decisionmaking power, the fewer women are found in such positions.

The gender-specific division of labor observed even in industrial countries takes on a far more rigid form in many developing ones. In the formal sector, most women are condemned to take unqualified jobs with low wages and no opportunities for promotion.[37] Most of the female workforce can still be found in the "informal sector," where working conditions are unprotected.

Such discrimination is not only unfair: it is also absurd from a development point of view. According to United Nations Population Fund, the rate of economic growth in areas where women enjoy greater social status is higher and the quality of life increases faster than in areas where women are disadvantaged.[38] In addition, there are many indications that women's income-generating activities have a highly desirable impact on the family, because women manage their incomes more sensibly than men. They use most of the money they earn for children, household services, and dietary improvements, while men often seem to succumb to the temptation of superficial consumer goods.[39] Thus, in Africa it is not unusual to see increasing malnutrition among children while male family members buy wristwatches, radios, mopeds, bicycles, alcohol, and so on.[40] The relationship between malnutrition and the diversion of family incomes by men for their personal consumption has been recognized as a major problem in Belize, Guatemala, Mexico, and the entire Indian subcontinent.[41]

There is no overall blueprint for the advancement of women in the developing world. Not only do the roles of women, their opportunities for self-determination, the social order, and economic and social conditions vary from country to country and from one ethnic group to the other, but regional differences also exist. Yet no one today would deny that merely using women as instruments is incompatible with a reasonable population policy and with sustainable development. Development policy that incorporates equity for women is a matter of common sense.

It is also a key to increased food security. Women in developing countries play significant roles in producing food and providing the income that goes toward the purchase of a family's food.[42] Numerous studies have documented that women account for 70–80 percent of household food production in sub-Saharan Africa, 65 percent in Asia, and 45 percent in Latin America and the Caribbean.[43] If they are given the same access to resources as men, women farmers post crop yields at least as high as their male counterparts. Other studies have shown that women tend to spend a higher share of any income they earn on food for the family. And their incomes are more closely associated than men's with better health and nutrition for their children.[44]

In an overview of women's important role in household food security, Agnes Quisumbing and colleagues at the International Food Policy Research Institute make the following recommendations:

> To allow women to fulfill their potential in generating food security, national governments and international organizations must take policy steps in three broad areas. First, they must increase women's physical and human capital. Women's ability to produce food can be enhanced by improving their access to resources, technology, and information. Literacy training for women and increased education for girls will increase productivity both today and in the future. Second, policymakers must increase women's ability to generate income to maximize the benefits of women's incomes for household food security and nutrition. Strategies should aim to increase women's productivity both in paid work and in domestic production, so women can increase their incomes without sacrificing additional time, their children's welfare, or their own health and nutritional status. Third, they must protect women's health and nutritional status to allow women to fulfill their productive and reproductive roles. Development or safety-net programs for women should increase women's income-earning potential while reducing the energy or time intensity of their activities. Other programs should address girls' and women's specific health needs and empower women to seek health care for themselves and for those who depend on them for food and nutrition security.[45]

Development activities that invest in women and give them access to land titles, credits, and the chance for employment with fair wages increase their freedom of action and their opportunities for self-fulfillment beyond their traditional roles. Such activities also ensure greater economic and social independence for women and more freedom of decision, thus enabling them to exercise their civil and political rights, including reproductive rights. In countries where birth rates have declined faster than expected given overall economic development, the explanatory factor has been the status of women in society: where this status is high, birth rates fall faster and in a more sustained way. This is why decreasing birth rates in Sri Lanka and in the Indian state of Kerala can be attributed to an increase in the marriageable age for women—which in turn is the result of improved educational and professional opportunities for girls and women.

When women are accepted as partners with equal rights in developing countries, a further long-term decline in birth rates can be expected. In societies where women depend greatly on men, sons are needed to provide social security for elderly parents. This means couples have roughly twice as many children. When women have the same social status as men and are economically independent, both men and women can help their parents have an adequate livelihood in old age, especially if they are disabled. When this is the case, empirical studies show that birth rates decrease.[46] Yet it would be intolerably one-sided for a male paradigm of modernization to define "progressive" women only as women who have fewer children, as sometimes seems to be the case. It is true that strengthening the social role of women has a positive impact on demography, but it can also provide impulses to general social development.

Criticism of gender relations and demands for change must become a matter of common sense and of broad consensus in the international community. The Cairo Conference and the 1995 World Conference on Women in Beijing, and the programs of action adopted at these conferences, pointed out the forms of discrimination and inequity that still exist and called for them to be overcome. Development must be oriented toward the good of all human beings, not just men. Development of this sort can make sustainable improvements in a society's living conditions. As with many other circumstances related to development, however, this is well known but rarely put into practice.[47]

The Position of Children in Traditional Societies

Let us consider something obvious that often receives insufficient mention or is taken too little into account in discussions about population policy. Children are part of what makes human life worth living, and they have a right to love and to special protection by the community. It is degrading to measure the "value" of children exclusively in terms of economic, social, reproductive, or other utilitarian considerations.

Wherever the gods or God are believed to favor great fertility, high birth rates are more widely accepted. When this view prevails, children are regarded less as the result of a rational decision made by their parents than as a "gift of God" or a sign of divine providence to be received with pride and gratitude. This view explains why some African societies, for example, have not adopted the concept of a "sufficient" or intentionally "desired" number of children. The higher the number of children, the better the chances of being assured of divine benevolence.[48] Men and women who have many children enjoy greater social and moral prestige.[49]

Further quasi-religious obligations for children of both sexes arise from the relationship between the living and the dead. Where people believe that their dead are reincarnated in the form of children born later, a certain number of progeny is necessary simply to allow ancestors a chance to make the necessary transformation. Often, naming reveals the relationship that is felt to exist between a newborn and the deceased. The complex interrelations between the living and the dead in some religions also require that certain burial rituals, ceremonies, or sacrificial offerings be undertaken. If the souls of the deceased are to rest in peace, such rituals and offerings can only be conducted or granted by someone's own children—and often only by sons.[50] This is why some cultures consider intentional limitation of fertility as a lack of respect for elders or deceased ancestors.

Because poverty consists of more than material deprivation, it can intensify the emotional and intrinsic value of parenthood. Poverty expresses itself just as strongly in the feeling of helplessness and complete unworthiness. The desire to have children can be reinforced by such feelings. Children are often the only "treasure" poor people have; children are a source of self-respect and hope for the future. Today these immaterial aspects of parenthood are often consciously expressed only in religious pronouncements. But they should be part and parcel of any serious analysis of population policy.

Some segments of society feel that infertility or a small number of children—sometimes the result of conscious family planning, sometimes a person's fate due to illness—are signs of individual bad luck or of serious deviation from social norms. In both cases, the persons affected may be punished, sometimes by violent sanctions.[51] Wherever the decision to have children is understood as something complex—determined by religion, culture, and society—government family planning policies may risk being perceived and rejected as immoral meddling in family privacy.[52] This perception arises especially when such policies are promoted by the West.

The fact that children provide emotional enrichment and the promise of immediate benefit only partly accounts for high birth rates, however. Having a greater number of children does not necessarily imply the existence of more love or attention. Often, the quality of life of existing children is diminished by the arrival of new children, increasing a family's misery. It is not true that every child is a "love child": the serious violations of human rights and the violence and brutality to which millions of children are exposed worldwide, day after day, suggest another truth.

Children as "Social Security" and "Health Insurance"

Wherever the state and its institutions lack credibility, or wherever modern insurance systems are not yet in a position to offer universal old-age pensions and sufficient health care in case of illness, the elderly and sick are cared for by their families. This system of care is motivated on the one hand by familial affection and feelings of duty, and on the other by intergenerational justice. In many parts of the developing world, children still assume such duties—for obvious psychological and institutional reasons. Until the beginning of the modern age, this was also the case in what are now the industrial countries.

Developing countries typically lack properly functioning capital markets and banking infrastructure that could absorb possible savings and invest them safely. Moreover, many developing countries have high annual inflation rates. As a result there is no guarantee of long-term security based on the savings that individuals may be able to accumulate for their old age. In many Asian countries, people have had to accept great losses after the outbreak of financial crises.

The state becomes an additional problem when its citizens consider it a menace rather than a trustworthy defender of public welfare and a guarantor of law and order. In everyday reality, the laxness, arbitrariness, and corruption of state employees and other people who have social and political power can prevent citizens from asserting their legitimate rights. Examples of such corruption—such as the recent one in which funds accumulated for the pensions of war veterans were used to finance a presidential family's exclusively private expenditures—are not hard to find.

Political unrest and violent changes of government certainly help convince people that they can only rely on themselves and their immediate families. It is not surprising that 80–90 percent of parents interviewed in Indonesia, Korea, the Philippines, Thailand, and even Turkey expected to be supported by their children in their old age.[53]

In societies where daughters become part of their husbands' families after marriage, as in many Asian and African countries, women need to have sons, not just children, to support parents in their old age. This quickly leads to having twice the number of children needed. Under such social circumstances, the position of the newly wedded woman within the family as well as her rights, her duties, and the quality of the tasks she is assigned depend on the number of children (sons) she has. As a result, she will want to have as many children as possible. Though the situation has clearly improved in the past 30 years, in many developing countries infant and child mortality is still so high that one additional child constitutes a relatively small "insurance premium," especially since another child in the family means relatively low additional costs.

However, the process of modernization now taking place in developing countries also erodes the sense that it is natural to look after parents when they become older. Many young people—especially those in an urban environment—no longer feel bound to traditional ways and customs. Moreover, the role of women is changing, and traditional patterns of division of labor are dissolving (such as the daughter-in-law looking after her husband's parents). In developing countries, women are now more likely to work outside the home and can thus no longer take over duties involving extensive care of family members even if they want to.

Finally, in view of more modern and individualistic lifestyles, growing urbanization, and high unemployment rates, an increasing number of parents are learning to acknowledge that to have many children no longer guarantees support in old age. Under these changed circumstances, it can actually be more profitable to have fewer but better-educated children.

Children as an "Economic Factor"

There is no generally accepted methodology or standard procedure for measuring the "economic benefit" of a child, but there are many indications that children are a great help and therefore a significant economic factor in family life.[54] Of course, children are a more important source of labor in rural areas and in households with primitive technical equipment than they are in cities; they are also more indispensable for the lower classes than the upper classes.[55] At this point, it is important to underline the distinction between child work and child labor.[56]

In every developing country, children do many different tasks, beginning when they are very young, especially in rural households (see Table 5).

Children's help is of most significance to their mothers, since children typically take up some of the many tasks that are usually considered women's duties. Children also often look after their younger siblings. Their duties therefore change as they get older, becoming increasingly demanding.

Child occupations of this kind have always existed, and they also still exist today in industrial countries. Children on farms grow up doing chores and are quite naturally accustomed to taking over a variety of tasks, as are the children of parents who have a workshop or their own business. According to the *World Development Report*, boys and girls aged six to eight work 3–4 hours a day in villages in Nepal. In Indonesia (Java), young people work 8–10 hours a day, and many children in Bangladesh work even longer.[57] In their study of rural regions in the Philippines, E.M. King and R.E. Evenson found that children in these areas indirectly contribute up to 20 percent of their families' incomes and approximately one third of the household production.[58] Other sources claim that older children indirectly con-

Table 5   Productive Activities of Children, According to Age Groups

Age group	Activities
5 to 9 years old	Guarding livestock (with older siblings); carrying water; going on small errands; collecting dung, dry grass, and wood; preparing food (cutting, peeling, etc.).
9 to 12 years old	Spinning, knitting, crocheting, milking cows, collecting fodder, guarding livestock (alone), buying goods on the market, running important errands, helping with the laundry.
12 to 15 years old	Selling goods on the market, doing errands in town, manuring, planting, harvesting, weeding, weaving, sewing, cooking.
15 years and older	Chopping wood; building and repairing fences, huts, and walls; shearing sheep.

tribute just as much toward household revenue as adults.[59] Normally, children's wages are significantly lower than the wages of adults, even under conditions of legitimate employment. Children are thus an attractive economic factor.[60]

In many cases, children also make things easier for older family members (particularly men) who delegate to children the tasks that they themselves find burdensome or feel they can no longer reasonably do. By gaining time in this way, adults can take on other jobs and perhaps earn additional revenue.

As social modernization gradually takes place, the economic significance of child work diminishes. At the same time, the cost of raising children increases. Both factors change the cost-benefit ratio that applies to children and reduce the incentive to have more children.

Child work of this kind is not objectionable as long as children perform tasks of their own free will, the physical demands of work are not excessive, and children are given a necessary minimum of free time to play. It is particularly important that child work does not hamper or prevent children from attending school. But are these conditions actually fulfilled? What child "freely" takes on tasks? In many cases it is hard to draw the line between acceptable and unacceptable child work. The boundary is a fluid one, especially in the case of absolute poverty.

It is quite obvious that child labor is closely linked to poverty: where poverty is severe, children must contribute to their family's income. Usually the children of rich parents do not need to work; when they take a job, they do so of their own free will. The kind of work done by children also depends on their parents' income: the poorest usually have to slave away under appalling working conditions. The higher the parents' social status, the more agreeable the jobs held by their children. Dirty and intolerable forms of child labor will only cease to exist when the poverty on which they are based is eradicated.

The tasks defined as child labor and those defined as child work show a number of similarities, but there is a major difference: child labor is done for money and outside the family home. It can consist of unskilled jobs such as cleaning, tidying up, packing things, and doing other odd jobs, but it can also consist of dirty, dangerous, and exhausting work in processing industries. In many cases, not only is child labor—sometimes consisting of part-time and well-paid jobs—a source of significant income for households living in absolute destitution; it can also promote and strengthen the position of children within the household.

Is child labor legitimate or should it be condemned? In assessing the acceptability of child labor, the same criteria should initially be used as for child work: it is tolerable as long as children work (more or less) of their own free will, the work does not make excessive physical demands, the children have a necessary minimum of leisure time, and the work does not hamper or prevent their education. As the work is performed for others and for money, however, an additional factor must be included in the debate: the issue of fair wages.

Child labor is no longer legitimate when children receive only a tiny proportion of the wages that adults get for the same work. Nor is it acceptable when the maximum legal working time is exceeded, when weekends are not free, and when no holidays are granted. Analyses of child labor should also include a discussion of the issues of health care and other social benefits—but without using industrial countries as a standard (for seen from this perspective, most adults in developing countries are probably not employed under legitimate conditions either).

Children are exploited whenever they are deprived of fair wages and decent working conditions or made to perform work that violates codes of morality. Working in the sex industry is not the only immoral form of child labor. Giving children health-endangering jobs simply because only people of small stature can do the work (such as cleaning the inside of sewage pipes) is also immoral.

Sometimes it is hard to prosecute exploitative employers because they hide behind alleged "apprenticeship contracts." In order to avoid paying fair wages, these employers argue that they are offering "training programs" and that children benefit much more than their employers. Further excuses include claims of "family or fostering arrangements" or "free board and lodging arrangements." In reality, physical and psychological pressure is exerted on children in many cases in order to keep them from taking the initiative to complain. Children often cannot file complaints anyway because corrupt institutions refuse to receive and process them. When parents are bound to their children's employer through debt, children are exploited for many years as unprotected slave laborers to pay off the interest on the debts. These types of exploitation are illegal in most developing countries, as they are in industrial countries. But legal processes are to no avail where no plaintiff exists. And where there is no plaintiff, there can be no defendant.

Nevertheless, the increasingly public debate over human rights is a source of hope. Pressure is being put on businesses in developing countries that have no scruples about enriching themselves by exploiting children. Another source of hope is the fact that a growing number of consumers are protesting against the exploitation of children by buying only products with "child-friendly" labels.

But if all facets of the problem of child labor are actually considered, it is not easy to justify a call for general prohibition. Solutions must be adapted to the structure of the problem and must always focus primarily on the child's well-being, or else good intentions will often result in the opposite of "good," as the United States discovered. Some years ago the U.S. Congress decided to combat child labor by removing the most-favored-nation clause from tariff agreements with countries in which it was legal to employ children.

Many American textiles are made in South Asian and South American countries. After Congress approved this resolution, many businesses in Bangladesh dismissed employees. This action affected girls who folded clothes and packed them in tissue paper at the end of production lines. These girls held relatively well-paid jobs (60 *thaka* per day, about $1.50). Their working environment was clean and protected against the weather. A subsequent investigation revealed that none of the girls dismissed went to a training school or received any other form of further education after having been made redundant. About 70 percent of them took on other jobs, such as breaking up stones for road construction, carrying sand for house construction, or similarly strenuous work. The work was much more physically demanding, and it had to be done outdoors without protection against the burning heat; moreover, at 30 *thaka* per day, the wages were also considerably lower than what they had previously earned. The rest of the girls found jobs in "bars" or went directly into prostitution.

The Levi-Strauss company found a much more prudent and sensitive way of protecting the interests of children. The firm analyzed the situation case-by-case, often taking over the costs of absence from work due to school attendance, and tried to re-employ children in better positions after they had finished school. The child's well-being was used as the standard of measure in these programs.

Bangladesh has undertaken a Food for Schooling program, designed to change the incentives for families deciding whether to send their children to work or to school. The program provides a free ration of food to poor families as long as primary school-age children attend school. By sending children to school, families earn grain that can be used to feed all family members, young and old, or they can sell the grain for cash to buy other needed goods such as clothing or medicine.[61]

Children and Human Rights

Human beings acquire their basic outlook on life during childhood, and the ways in which they confront life are also shaped at this time. When children live on the social and economic margins of society and when they know only poverty, misery, discrimination, and abuse, this influences their lives as adults. But if society ensures the freedom and dignity of children and creates conditions that allow them to develop their capacities, there is a chance that they will grow up to be reasonable and content human beings who can accept social responsibility.

In most societies, children's physical and mental immaturity makes them almost completely dependent on the political and economic power structures of adults for protection of their rights and their well-being.[62] Yet instead of receiving special protection, children often find that their dependence and vulnerability are exploited by those in positions of responsibility—in the name of economic necessity, culture, or tradition. Children are considered property, and their individual rights are subordinated to the interests of the family, the community, and the authorities.

The range of human rights violations against children exceeds the scope of this book, but it certainly exceeds what is imaginable within the bounds of human decency. It extends from disregard of children's basic needs to physical and mental cruelty, sexual abuse, rape, prostitution, trafficking, detainment, torture, kidnapping, and even homicide and murder. Just a few aspects of the problem are discussed here.

The degree to which children are defenseless depends to a great extent on aspects of their identity, such as sex, ethnic origin, caste, or economic status. But defenselessness is part of a wider context of discrimination, want, and disadvantage in much of the world, particularly South America, and probably most of all in Asia. In South Asia, children make up 40 percent of the population (approximately 612 million of more than 1.5 billion people are under the age of 18, and 12 percent of the total population is under the age of 5). Altogether, more than one fourth of all the children in the world live in South Asia. Their experiences in life are an important gauge not only of the status of human rights in South Asia, but also of the conditions of life for children worldwide.

Violations of children's rights are related to the general disadvantages suffered by children in terms of economic and social rights. According to UNICEF, every year 4.7 million children under 5 die of illnesses that can largely be prevented and cured, such as diarrhea and respiratory tract diseases. Two thirds of the surviving children are undernourished. Urbanization, poverty, and the disintegration of families have made millions of children homeless or have forced children to fend for themselves. They eke out a living on the streets—precisely where they are most exposed to violence and exploitation. Girls or children who belong to marginal groups experience additional discrimination and social disadvantage.

Girls in South Asia are disadvantaged in another way. Since the birth of a girl is still considered a burden for the family, parents invest less in the health and education of girls than of boys. Citing the Koran, the Muslim fundamentalist Taliban rulers of Afghanistan even denied girls the right to education. When girls are denied education because they happen to be girls or because they live in poverty, and when they are also compelled to work, they are consigned to a cycle of ostracism and powerlessness that leads to further violations of their civil, political, economic, social, and cultural rights. In many countries, the abortion of a female fetus and the murder of female infants are nothing out of the ordinary.

Statistics on mortality and illiteracy reflect a high percentage of girls. Together with other damaging practices, such as the payment of dowries and child marriage, these conditions offer fertile ground for a continual cycle of domestic violence and sexual exploitation. Treating girls in such a discriminatory way increases the marginalization of women and leads to problems being handed down from one generation to the next.

Traditional practices reflect this discrimination and the low social status of women and girls. For example, the traditional customs of the *devadasi* in India not only serve to maintain systems for smuggling and enslaving women and girls; they also include the ritual marriage of girls to divinities. Later the girls are often sold into forced prostitution. In the *deukis* system in Nepal, rich families who have no daughters buy young girls from poor communities and make offerings of them in temples as if they were their own. These girls are not allowed to marry and often end up as mistresses or prostitutes. The United Nations reported that 17,000 girls were donated as *deukis* in the year 1992.

These infringements of rights occur in a wider social context in which the tradition of child marriage weighs heavily upon girls. In many areas of South Asia, girls are married at a very early age, as their age and sexual innocence increase the bride price. Child marriage deprives girls of their childhood. It can become an emotional burden and cause psychological and physical health problems. Moreover, it makes girls powerless against the physical aggression committed by their husbands and in-laws.

The predicament of girls in South Asia is often exacerbated by the custom of dowry. What was devised as a form of social security for women has become a means to acquire consumer goods and capital. The amount of the dowry paid for a woman is determined by both families as part of the marriage contract. In some communities, the low status of girls implies that the dowry is paid to the husband's parents by the bride's parents during the marriage ceremony. Conflicts over payment of dowries often lead to domestic violence and other crimes such as rape, mutilation, starvation, and even murder (often by burning).

Deplorable economic conditions, social ostracism, and political marginalization, combined with the vulnerability of children and young people, contribute to further abuse. It is no surprise that in India, for example, children from the lowest castes, the so-called *dalits*, constitute the majority of child workers in bonded labor. Furthermore, in the conflicts in Afghanistan and Sri Lanka, children were persecuted because of their ethnic identity. Everywhere in South Asia, children are thrown into prison because they try to fend for themselves outside the context of families or social networks.

The experiences of poor and underprivileged children force us to remember that human rights are indivisible. When children lack economic, social, and cultural rights, their chances of exercising their civil and political rights are severely restricted. Freedom to organize your own life and the life of the community is necessary to attain human dignity. Human beings can only accomplish this if they can enjoy fundamental human rights that guarantee their intellectual, moral, and physical existence and development. Among these are the right to life and security of person; the right to self-development; the right to freedom of thought, conscience, and religion; the right to express opinions freely; and the right to freedom of peaceful assembly and association. Since these and other rights are essential prerequisites for a life of dignity, they are acknowledged as natural human rights to which all human beings are equally entitled; moreover, these rights are defined as inviolable and inalienable.

Chapter 7

Prerequisites for Responsible Population Policies

You do not need to be a religious believer or a philosopher to recognize that an ethical perspective must be brought to bear on population policy. After all, human life is at stake. Like other types of policy, population and food policies can be guided by ethical principles. They are not at the mercy of any particular ideology or set of circumstances—especially when seen in a global context. Although the discussion here focuses on the human dimensions of population and food policies, it is not meant as a moral admonition. Yet we admit at the outset that the observations made here reflect our own views of the issues as well as our personal value judgments.

Putting Our Ecological Houses in Order

A discussion of global environmental stresses and risks needs to address a wide range of factors—everything from the use of nuclear power, the spread of AIDS, and the release of transgenic plants to the increasingly acute greenhouse effect and the destabilization of the global ecosystem. Once again, due to the complex origins and nature of global environmental problems, a single solution is out of the question. Population growth alone has never caused environmental problems: forms of resource deployment and consumption as well as technological advances have always played a key role. Consequently, the impact of population growth, consumer behavior, and production models can only be assessed within an analytical system that incorporates circular interdependencies.[1] Major research efforts are still required to design such a system.

One approach to capturing these interdependencies is the concept of "environmental space." First, an acceptable level of per capita consumption or per capita

97

emissions is calculated for various resource and emission categories (such as carbon dioxide [CO_2]) and compared with the value for the current year and a future target year (2010, for example). If the real current value or the estimated future annual value exceed the acceptable value, per capita consumption and emissions must be reduced by a corresponding percentage in order to ensure sustainability and equality.

Since the greenhouse effect represents probably the greatest threat to future development and since anthropogenic influences on the climate are increasingly dominated by CO_2, the following example should illustrate the concept.[2] It is currently assumed that the oceans and biosphere absorb around 14 billion tons of carbon dioxide a year. To prevent any further increase in CO_2 concentration in the atmosphere, one characteristic of a sustainable development strategy should be a commitment to restricting global CO_2 emissions to around 14 billion tons a year. This is slightly more than half the current volume of emissions. For 1995 the World Resources Institute estimated a total CO_2 emission level of around 22.7 billion tons from industry and traffic.[3] Added to this, 3.4 billion tons are accounted for by burn clearance.[4] Assuming that the industrial and traffic-related emissions make up approximately 80 percent of CO_2 levels, the release of carbon dioxide is currently 27–28 billion tons—or double the threshold value from a sustainability standpoint.

Based on the equality premise, everyone in the world is due approximately 2.3 tons a year of CO_2 (14 billion tons of CO_2 divided by 6 billion), and only 2 tons of CO_2 per person for an estimated population of 6.9 billion in 2010.[5] Yet actual national statistics show CO_2 emissions per person in Germany at 10.2 tons a year and in the United States at more than 20 tons.[6] People in Africa or India, on the other hand, are responsible for only 1 ton of emissions per person a year, while people in China are slightly over the "environmental space" quota at 2.7 tons per head.

If we add a qualitative ecological dimension to this quantitative population analysis and include not just numbers of people but their impact on the environment (approximated by the industrial CO_2 emissions), the weighting shifts dramatically. Comparing India and Germany, for example, shows that Germany's 82 million people have the same total environmental impact as 836 million Indians, in terms of CO_2 emissions, since the Germans produce 10.2 times the level of CO_2 emissions per person.[7] Applying the same methodology to China and the United States, then 272 million U.S. citizens would be equivalent to more than 2 billion Chinese.

Industrial countries now account for less than 20 percent of the world's population yet are responsible for two thirds of global energy consumption. The per capita consumption of energy (as an indicator for CO_2 emissions) in industrial countries is high and rising, albeit slowly. In developing countries the per capita consumption of energy is still low but rising rapidly because of population growth and continuing modernization. At present, CO_2 emissions in developing countries are responsible for one third of global emissions, but this figure is expected to increase to around 45 percent over the next 10 years.[8] High population growth, increasing urbanization, and the growing demand for individual mobility are driving this trend; yet in 30 years' time the per capita consumption of energy in developing countries will still be only one fifth the current level in industrial countries.

In terms of "sustainable development," all the world's countries are still developing, as none has achieved the goal of sustainability in all its activities. The credibility of industrial countries' didactic statements on the strain that population growth places on global sustainability depends on their efforts to put their own ecological houses in order. The move to reverse the trend toward rising per capita energy consumption and to mitigate global risks such as climate change must come from industrial countries.

Basic Development Goals

After being influenced for the last 40 years by the assumption that economic growth would almost automatically lead to development and social progress, development cooperation at the end of the twentieth century—in theory as well as practice—once again began to focus on meeting basic needs. This term now includes more than the basic needs that were the focus of development assistance in the seventies, however. Development is now concerned not only with practical needs such as food security, basic health, and clean drinking water, but also with so-called strategic needs, including human rights, gender equality, and the development of civil society.

It has become clear that income, while important, is only one of the things that human beings wish to have at their disposal. Income is only a means to an end— the fulfillment of human development. All human beings should have the following three possibilities in life:

- the chance to lead a healthy and fulfilling life,

- the chance to acquire knowledge and skills, and

- the chance to have reliable access to the resources they need for a decent standard of living.

But human development involves considerably more than these possibilities. The chance to enjoy political, economic, and social freedom, the opportunity to be creative and productive, and the chance to lead a life of self-esteem with a guarantee of human rights are also of great importance to many people.

Development policy must be much more clearly tailored to the interests of the poor in developing countries. Effective development and population policies require far-reaching change in old-age insurance schemes, in the advancement of women, in education, and in health care. Support for family planning methods that respect the freedom and the responsibility of couples in developing countries will also be necessary.

Human-centered policies that promote sustainable development offer people hope for the future. This is an essential prerequisite for development policies in general, and for population policies in particular. Hope is a liberating source of motivation that inspires people to take action to secure a better future.

The quality of development goals must be reflected in the quality of the means and the methods used in population policies. Population policy begins with the fundamentals: Even though population growth in many developing countries will continue to be reduced by deaths resulting from civil wars, climatic extremes, and political negligence, under no circumstances must these factors be seen as possible "solutions" to the problem of high population. Nor must they be advocated as a way of controlling population growth.[9] For ethical reasons, as well as for reasons of general social development, measures that actively seek to reduce high population growth must focus exclusively on lowering the birth rate.

High population growth can also threaten human values. Therefore, intervention of some sort may be necessary to protect against or reduce harm to present and future generations. On the other hand, governmental interference with the right of parents to voluntarily determine the number of children they have also constitutes a threat to human values. There is no easy solution to this ethical dilemma. The ongoing search for appropriate procedures is a search for the lesser evil. Accordingly, the options must be examined by first answering the following questions:[10]

- What human good and what values should be pursued or maintained—that is, what are the aims of population policy?

- What range of methods and activities is compatible with these aims—that is, what resources are appropriate to achieve the aims of population policy?

- What procedures and what reasons underlie the decisions we make about aims and resources, and about the ways they interrelate in a specific situation—that is, what ethical criteria should be used in decisionmaking?

The Aims of Population Policy

Population policy is one component of sustainable, human-centered development policies; as such, it is subordinate to the aims of development policies. This was made clear in the basic principles of the Programme of Action adopted in 1994 by the International Conference on Population and Development in Cairo.[11] According to this program, reproductive health and family planning methods should be considered in light of the following principles:

- The Universal Declaration of Human Rights is to be observed at all times, particularly the rights to life, liberty, and individual security.

- Human beings should be at the center of efforts to promote sustainable development and have the right to a healthy, productive life in harmony with nature.

- The right to development is a universal and inalienable human right.

- The following should be the cornerstones of programs concerned with population and development: support for equal rights, gender equality, and empowerment of women; elimination of all forms of violence against women; and guarantees for women of freedom of choice concerning regulation of their own fertility.

- Governments have an obligation to work toward the elimination of poverty, the equitable allocation of resources, and conservation of the environment and to support the right of all people to have an education.

Population policy has an impact on the most intimate sphere of human activity: reproductive behavior. The right of parents to determine the number of children they have will be affected to varying degrees, depending on how a country's population policy is constituted. Interventions of this sort require ethical consent at both the social and the individual level. One reason for this need for consent is the general need to protect the freedom of the individual from state interference and social pressure. Another is that human life and human values are at stake—at least wherever abortion comes into play as a factor in regulating the birth rate. Discussions based exclusively on statistical considerations do not fulfill the requirements for humane population policy. *The aim of all population policy measures is not to stabilize the population at a certain level or reduce birth rates per se, but to improve the quality of life for people living in a society where these measures are being applied.*

Pursuit of racial, social, geopolitical, or other utilitarian aims—such as ensuring material possessions or the political hegemony of particular countries or social groups—is not compatible with ethical population policies.[12] Equally incompatible is encouragement or prevention of human life in accordance with certain standards of "quality."[13]

Legitimate population policy aims are linked with the economic, social, and ecological consequences of high population growth, which combine to retard sustainable development and pose a direct threat to present and future generations. Obviously, the pace of population growth is already outstripping the capacity of governments to provide adequate services, social programs, and infrastructure. Continued population growth makes it more difficult to solve all other problems. At least since the time of the Cairo Conference, there has been a global consensus about the primary aim of a humane population policy: it must enable a society to follow a course toward sustainable development, to facilitate this course, and to accelerate the requisite processes.

A population policy is "ethically acceptable" if it acknowledges that all human beings are equal in terms of human dignity and if it reduces human suffering and injustice while promoting freedom, equity, and opportunity. Long-term satisfaction of basic human needs as well as implementation of social goals under conditions of dignity and freedom are of paramount importance. A policy conceived along these lines will be underpinned by respect for life, in the sense that Albert Schweitzer used this term: it will preserve and advance life and enhance its value to the utmost.[14] "Life" in this sense also includes future generations. A population policy must therefore aim to create the social conditions that motivate parents to take the responsibility for voluntary decisions about family size to a level compatible with sustainable development—while also keeping the general public welfare in mind. Any option for reducing a country's birth rate through voluntary developmental and sociopolitical means must be given precedence over government programs to limit population growth, particularly when they involve coercive measures.

The following are prerequisites for an ethically acceptable population policy:[15]

- avoidance of unwanted pregnancies and the consequences associated with them, particularly impacts on the health and future development of mothers;

- avoidance or at least reduction of induced abortions resulting from unwanted pregnancies;

- development of more effective health care systems and improvements in national health;

- prevention or at least retardation of the spread of sexually transmitted diseases, especially AIDS;

- more equitable gender relations through enhancement of the social role of women; and

- encouragement of mutual understanding and active partnerships between men and women as well as between generations.

Ethical Decisionmaking Criteria for Legitimate Government Measures

A thoroughgoing discussion of whether and how to intervene in the reproductive decisions of a family calls for considerable interdisciplinary analysis. Like any other question that concerns human life, the question of human reproduction cannot be examined only from a biological, psychological, demographic, sociological, or legal point of view. The integrity and uniqueness of the human being must always be at the center of any debate over human reproduction.

Official population policies that are legitimate in ethical terms must be based on respect for human life. The inviolable dignity of human life and the fundamental right to life are not psychological, physical, or intellectual achievements, and they are certainly not tied to gender. Human life is not shaped by external decrees or purposes; it is self-constituting at every stage of development. The right to reproduce life, like the right to life itself, is inviolable and inalienable, and belongs to all human beings by virtue of their individual human dignity. Human rights are a basic birthright to which every person is entitled regardless of his or her social status, religious affiliation, or classification according to any other social criteria.

In 1948 the United Nations adopted the Universal Declaration of Human Rights, a catalogue of inalienable rights to which all human beings are entitled. In addition to the right to life and the right to reproduce, the Declaration includes the following that are relevant to discussions of population policy:

- the right to freedom and security of the individual person,

- the right to equality before the law,

- the right to protection from interference in private life and family life,

- the right of families and children to special protection,

- the right to freedom of conscience and freedom of religion,

- the right to social security and free development of personality, and

- the right of women to protection against discrimination.

Many countries have incorporated the rights listed in the Declaration into their own national law, usually as "fundamental rights" guaranteed in the constitution. Despite acceptance of the universal applicability of these fundamental human rights, interpreting their meaning and putting them into practice still depend largely on the particular political, religious, and cultural features of different societies. Thus, for example, societies that place a high value on individualism (as most Western democracies do) interpret the "right to life" differently than societies that emphasize social consensus or societies with totalitarian governments. These differences affect what individual couples are permitted to do, as well as influence the burdens they face in the context of population policy.

Historical experience shows that totalitarian states have generally taken a different view of human rights than democratically constituted states. The policies and actions of totalitarian regimes are not subject to the approval of voters. Even now, at the beginning of the twenty-first century, fundamentalist religious minorities in political power use the authority of religion to deny women their fundamental human rights. Guarantees of human rights may be regarded by some states as an "internal matter." But human rights are merely recognized or not recognized by the state; they are not created by the state. Moreover, as the debate over NATO intervention in Kosovo revealed, the power of "sovereignty" must not be used to deny the legitimate rights of those who granted sovereignty in the first place—the people who live within the borders of the state.

Extensions of state power into the realm of private life must not be taken lightly. The use of political coercion or other types of force to curtail or deny the right to decide freely and responsibly how many children to have amounts to more than a mere violation of social norms: it constitutes a violation of human rights. What is more, the use of state power to this end does not accomplish its intended aim.

Official population policies that are not based on the consent of the great majority of people in a society will have little chance of lasting success. Many studies show that official coercion or even compulsory measures have definite limits wherever the desire to have fewer children has not yet been internalized. Ethically legitimate population policies are based on the informed consent of the people affected, with respect to measures used, individual freedom of decision, and the type of contraceptive devices employed. Mandatory programs, by contrast, must be enforced through continual coercion. This results in a "Stalinization" of population policy, whereby enforced success collapses when the level of coercion is reduced or when official pressure can no longer be maintained. Moreover, coercion and compulsory measures instituted by the state in the past have done severe long-term damage to the concept of family planning (as in India in the seventies).

Priority must therefore be given to all policy measures that serve to improve the quality of human life. This approach is a prerequisite for the type of informed parenthood, involving voluntary responsibility, that is compatible with long-term development options. Policies that take account of not only self-interest but also the interests of others will find greater acceptance in any society than policies that merely focus on maximizing specific self-interest in the short term.

In cases where the state is compelled to institute policies limiting the number of births to avoid some greater evil, this must be done under certain conditions: there must be a focus on human development, optimal implementation of human rights, and protection of the individual right to conduct social affairs in freedom and dignity.[16] Because obvious conflicts will arise over observance of human rights in such extreme cases, the state has an obligation to act so as to ensure that all restrictions on human rights are limited in time and that violations of human rights are minimized as far as possible. Official population policies designed to limit the birth rate must always represent a choice of the lesser evil, following a careful examination of alternatives.

Ethical Dilemmas

In some situations it is necessary to choose between two or more courses of action, each of which is associated with a certain degree of guilt over failure to observe established moral codes. There may be no concrete choice between action that is ethically acceptable and action that is ethically unacceptable, but merely a choice between two or more evils. In addition, failure to act, or continuing to tolerate a particularly difficult situation, may also be unethical. At this point, there is a need to be guided by the "lesser evil."

In principle, ethical values and norms should not become the object of agreements. Nor is it possible for unethical activity to become "relatively" ethical, even if it is perceived as expedient. Whereas an individual can refuse to take an unethical course of action, governments, because of their responsibility to act on behalf of others, are obligated in situations of conflict to consider alternatives carefully, with the goal of finding optimal, or least objectionable, solutions. Ethical dilemmas are a permanent part of life beyond the context of population policy, but they must certainly be confronted there as well.

The Well-being of Present versus Future Generations

Some countries use the quality of life of future generations as a justification to urge or even compel people to limit the number of children they have. A rationale of this sort cannot simply be dismissed out of hand. In China, for instance, it must be noted in all fairness that unrestricted population growth would have caused major ecological problems and enormous bottlenecks in food supply as well as in satisfaction of other basic needs.[17] Even today, less than one third of the global average of agricultural land per capita is available in China. Like the implementation of voluntary population policies, attempts to prevent future disasters also have an ethical character.

How much freedom of decision regarding reproduction can be guaranteed once a population has exceeded ecological, economic, and social carrying capacity? Once physical survival is no longer possible, freedom also becomes impossible—whether it is the freedom to reproduce or any other type. What course should be taken when guarantees of human dignity and the right to full development of personality for present generations clash with guarantees of human dignity and development of personality for future generations? Which should have priority? Is there any ethical justification—aside from a theological one—for demanding sacrifices from the present generation so that people still unborn who are alive 100 years from now might have a better life? These questions raise highly controversial moral issues—such as the nature of human beings or what objects can be appropriately considered in the context of morality.[18]

Questions such as these cannot be answered purely by arguments made on behalf of population policy without reference to moral philosophy. Of course, state intervention in the private life of the individual should always be a last resort, used only when all other less intrusive options for intervention have been exhausted. Once all such means of intervention have been tried without success, the argument of solidarity between generations must be introduced if present generations are to be asked to make sacrifices for the benefit of future generations. However, this argument involves considerable preparatory effort.

How we define morality will influence our attitude toward particular ethical circumstances. It will also determine whether a particular circumstance is considered from an ethical standpoint. A narrow perspective—for example, one that regards human sexuality only from a moral point of view—will omit consideration of such factors as social equity and environmental sustainability. Many people feel an intense responsibility to conserve vital natural resources for their own children and grandchildren. But advocating similar rights for anonymous future generations is much more difficult—especially under conditions of absolute poverty.

Individual Well-being versus the General Public Welfare

Children who give and receive love are a source of joy in human life. Depending on the social environment, children can also make substantial contributions to family livelihood and social security. Cultural and religious factors within a specific social context can additionally place a heavy obligation on parents to produce many children. These realities lead at least to some degree of conflict in the short term between individual well-being, arising from self-determination and pursuit of private interests, and the public welfare of present and future generations.

Garrett Hardin compares this situation with the tragedy of the commons (common land used by the entire community) in the case of nomadic herdsmen, who are caught in a system that forces them to enlarge their herds.[19] Wherever collective property, such as common pastures, forests, or water resources, is used in unorganized fashion by everyone, with no incentive to conserve, the community as a whole will pay a final price. The problematical environmental policy of externalizing costs on an individual or societal basis is of great relevance to population policy. In this regard, several factors are important in specific cases: whether externalization of the social costs of a high number of children is a conscious activity, an activity based on incomplete information, or an activity that excludes consideration of the consequences.

Long-term educational measures will be necessary in any event, as this is the only way to disseminate information about the social and ecological consequences of having many children and demonstrate the need to limit population growth. Maintaining that it is necessary to put limits on reproductive freedom in order to preserve other valuable freedoms in the long term may seem like extremely abstract reasoning to a nomadic family in the Sahel zone. But in view of the deterioration of vegetation on overused soils in the region, this message nonetheless needs to be conveyed.

Appeals to conscience or to social responsibility, however defined, are of as little use in effecting a turnaround in reproductive behavior as they are in effecting changes in environmental attitudes. As long as individual activity detrimental to the public welfare is advantageous for the individual (or is perceived as advantageous), such appeals may fall on deaf ears. Those who act with self-restraint based on their own insight and sense of responsibility may eventually become a minority that is unable to avert disaster.

In resolving conflicts between individual well-being and the public welfare, interference with individual rights is not automatically an illegitimate approach. But priority for the public welfare has become a matter of broad international consensus—albeit to varying degrees, depending on the country and the social order.[20] Thus it is possible to argue, in the context of population policy, that the unrestricted right to individual development of personality reaches its limits whenever it interferes with the basic rights of others.

In the past, subordination of individual rights to collective social purposes has been used as a pretext by totalitarian states to exploit and repress their citizenry or portions of it. The right of the state to restrict individual freedom must therefore be exercised only within a specifically defined political and legal framework. The minimum criterion is the existence of a legitimate democratic state that strives to promote the general public welfare on a cooperative basis and that is accountable for every aspect of its activity. Ideally, those responsible for public policy will conduct themselves in accordance with the "golden rule" of population policy—treating others as they would wish to be treated themselves. Policy guidelines of this sort do not entail unacceptable inequalities.

The only conceivable reason for limiting the human right to reproduce is protection against a greater social evil, be it ecological disaster, inadequate material bases for a life of dignity, mass poverty, or war-like conflicts over dwindling natural resources.

Abortion

Despite all the progress that has been made in reproductive health care and dissemination of family planning methods and resources, the United Nations Population Fund estimates that there are still 75–80 million unwanted pregnancies each year.[21] Experience indicates that unwanted pregnancies lead to abortions. Each year around 22 percent of 210 million pregnancies end in abortion. This amounts to about 45 million abortions per year, 126,000 per day, or more than one per second. Approximately 25 million of these abortions are legal, and roughly 20 million are illegal.[22] The numbers are especially high in developing countries: of 182 million pregnancies there per year, 36 percent are unplanned and 20 percent end in abortion.

Abortion is defined as termination of pregnancy and the development of embryonic life subsequent to the thirteenth day following conception, after the fertilized egg is implanted in the uterus.[23] After this point, the unborn life form is subject to legal protection in most societies. Abortion is generally considered immune from prosecution in cases where pregnancy would do intolerable physical or psychological harm to a woman (medical indications), where it is clear that a newborn infant would suffer irreversible damage (genetic indications), or where pregnancy is the result of a sexual offence (ethical indications).

Sociopolitical discussions of abortion in industrial countries usually cite the following as arguments in favor of legal abortion:

- the high number of illegal abortions and related risks to the health and dignity of women,

- the dilemma of women who face the threat of prosecution for terminating an unwanted pregnancy,

- the widespread lack of effectiveness of existing legal sanctions, and

- the right of women to self-determination.

Opponents of abortion believe that a woman's right to self-determination must be subordinate to the right of the unborn child and emphasize the right of the unborn to full legal protection. This view is in harmony with the constitutional guarantee of the fundamental right to life. Most opponents of abortion argue that the right to life should be extended to grant special protection to human life that is unaware, no longer aware, or not yet aware of its own rights.

In most industrial countries, abortion is legal only in cases where the life and the emotional and physical health of the mother or the child are in danger. There is no reason to apply any other standard in developing countries. In accordance with positions adopted at the Programme of Action at the Cairo Conference and the Fourth World Conference on Women in Beijing, abortion must not be used as a substitute for contraception or as a means of birth control. Any other course of action would constitute a double standard. If prohibition of abortion as an instrument of population policy is to amount to more than meaningless agitation and rhetoric characterized by a moralizing tone of disapproval, we must recognize a social obligation to guarantee the right to reproductive health as well as free access to institutions concerned with family planning.

Conclusion

In a world richer in terms of knowledge, experience, and material resources than any previous period in human history, efforts to promote sustainable development must not be debased by inhumane policies. Population policy that involves state intervention in reproductive behavior will only be ethically acceptable if the following conditions are met:[24]

- Couples and individuals must be guaranteed the human right to decide freely and responsibly the number and spacing of their children and have the information to ensure informed choices.

- Respect for the freedom of the individual must be embedded in respect for the freedom of others and therefore linked to the general welfare.

- Conflicts between individual self-development and protection of community rights should be resolved as far as possible on the basis of rational discourse.

- Official policies that aim to reduce a country's population growth should create a social and economic environment that allows individuals to perceive their personal interests with a sense of responsibility, while encouraging self-restraint in reproductive behavior as a rational course of action.

- When restrictions on individual freedom are unavoidable, they should apply to all members of society, not only to low-income groups and ethnic minorities.

- Couples must give their voluntary and informed consent to any means and measures used to promote contraception.

An ethical population policy will primarily aim to create social and economic conditions that motivate parents to decide—in a voluntary and responsible fashion that takes account of the general welfare—to limit the children they have to a number compatible with sustainable development. The main pillars of population policy "with a human face" are well known today.

Thus the Programme of Action adopted at the International Conference on Population and Development in Cairo put considerable emphasis on reproductive rights and reproductive health—for both women and men.[25] The Conference also emphasized the necessity of gender equality, responsible sexual behavior, and better access to appropriate information and services. There was general agreement that special efforts must be made to ensure that men also assume their share of responsibility for partnership with respect to

- the obligations of parenthood;

- changing their sexual and reproductive behavior, including in the area of family planning;

- the health of mother and child, before and after birth, and avoidance of risky pregnancies;

- prevention of sexually transmitted diseases, including AIDS;

- control over family income in collaboration with women;

- educating and training children and ensuring that the family is healthy and well fed; and

- equal recognition and support for children of both sexes.

Men must be part of the childrearing process at the earliest possible stage. Special attention should be given to preventing violence against women and children. This broad agenda aims to resolve all social and cultural problems that are crucial for reproductive health policy and programs associated with it.

Chapter 8

The Battle for a Better Future

A s noted in earlier chapters, we already know what type of population and food policies could deliver cost-effective success in an ethically acceptable and responsible manner. We also know the social, economic, ecological, political, and other parameters of sustainable development within which such policies must be embedded:

- a political environment that ensures good governance and effective economic, social, ecological, and political decisionmaking on development;

- ecologically sustainable and socially acceptable economic development (economic growth) that also offers notable benefits to lower-income brackets;

- efficient, effective, and low-cost food systems that are compatible with the sustainable use of natural resources;

- improvement in the social standing of women, particularly their legal, educational, and economic status;

- social security systems and pension schemes that render reliance on large families superfluous; and

- reliable and adequate supplies of safe, modern methods of family planning and contraception.

The tragedy of current deficits is not lack of knowledge but lack of the political will to apply knowledge. Hence "good governance" is essential not only to ensure

113

the quality of development and population policies, but also to achieve consistency and coherence in their implementation. The political will to translate into practice the binding conventions that almost all industrial and developing countries signed at Rio, Cairo, Beijing, and Rome leaves much to be desired. Here lies the rub. In countries where the political will has been mobilized and ministries and authorities are sufficiently motivated, significant progress has been made. Wherever the political will is lacking, progress has been nonexistent.[1]

The quality of the means must also be reflected in the quality of the ends. State mechanisms enforced on citizens—particularly mandatory abortions—are counterproductive to the welfare of future generations. Legitimate ends by no means legitimize illegal means.

The Pessimists and the Optimists

You have probably heard of the gruesome experiment that shows that a frog thrown into hot water will immediately jump out whereas a frog thrown into cold water that is slowly heated will stay in until the water is so hot the frog finally dies. This analogy is commonly used to describe human beings' reaction to the greenhouse effect. Optimists are convinced that people are not frogs and that, if it gets too hot, people will find some way of turning off the heat. Indeed, never before in human history have such technological quantum leaps been taken as in the last 200 years. These 200 years have generated more knowledge than all previous centuries, the past 100 years more than the previous century, and the past 25 years more than the previous quarter-century. Never before have so many resources been invested in research and development.

Against this background, the assumption that technical progress will continue to provide us with new options in the future is not overly optimistic. It may well be that we are overestimating the rate of technical progress over the next two years, but most of us underestimate the rate of technical progress over the next 10–20 years. The replacement of scarce resources with other products, as posited by the optimistic school of thought, is now a reality. And where scarcity has led to higher prices, an increase in supplies has occurred—as with the production of food since 1974. Leaving aside politically induced crises, poor governance, and human failings that have led to war and civil conflict, none of the catastrophes predicted in the late sixties and early seventies has come to pass.

Yet pessimistic predictions continue to find a high level of acceptance. Western societies have always taken bearers of bad news and scaremongers more seriously than prophets of a carefree future and harbingers of positive news. People in that part of the world appear to view the future more pessimistically and the "blessings" of technical progress with more skepticism than people elsewhere (for instance, in the developing countries of Asia). Frequently they view social change and technical innovation with a sense of disquiet, and the expected benefits are given less credence than the feared risks—witness the current debate on biotechnology and genetic engineering.

It is difficult to change this attitude, since people's ideas of what is realistic or unrealistic, what constitutes heaven or hell, what is probable or improbable, depend largely on subjective perceptions. It seems that many people seek a specific order in the course of everyday events. As soon as they perceive a specific order, they are able to affirm this particular worldview through selective attention. Those who see Earth and its human, animal, and vegetable inhabitants at risk will seek—and find—information that confirms this expectation. If concern for the future and skepticism vis-à-vis technology is the dominant feeling, the focus will be on the risks and dangers of change. In the process, opportunities are all too easily ignored. If, however, the individual believes that all problems are essentially solvable, empirical data can be found and a "can-do" attitude drives innovation, allowing solutions for existing problems to be devised.

As so often in life, the most extreme statements of both sides—the pessimists and the optimists—are wrong. Neither a blind and carefree faith in technology nor the "worst-case" school of thought is a good guide to reality. Yet both positions bring to the table ideas that are important to sustainable courses of development.

The strongest argument for the optimist school of thought is that shortages are manifested by price hikes, which serve as an incentive for social change and technical progress. Over the past 25 years, such technical progress has substantially changed our way of life:

- The latest Japanese computer games for children have more calculating capacity than the world-famous Cray computer of the early seventies, whose export was subject to the most rigorous controls in the interest of national security.

- Communications technology has so revolutionized life that in a few years it will be possible to transfer agrarian and health technologies at little expense to even the most remote regions of poor countries, through a type of "Internet café." Even now, more and more people are becoming electronic neighbors, thanks to the Internet. The world has become a global village.

- Agricultural research has produced new seed varieties of staple crops like rice that produce three to four times the yield of the best seed varieties of the seventies. Breakthroughs in wheat are imminent.

- Even now in the United States, boring technologies have enabled the production of geothermal energy (heat from Earth's core). The potential of this fuel source is 1,000 times greater than the coal reserves in the United States and would pose no additional threat to the climate.

- Scientists have made significant strides in developing wind energy and photovoltaic cells that enable the direct conversion of sunlight into electricity. The cost per watt of photovoltaic electricity dropped by a factor of 50 between 1973 and 1995.[2]

- The accomplishments of the more resource-efficient technologies are so overwhelming that it is surprising the impact has not spread further.[3]

- Good governance, including the full use of technological tools, is now the key variable for a global increase in the standard of living for the 3–5 billion persons who will be born during the next 100 years.[4]

Biotechnology: A Case Study on a Promising Technology

In recent years, the views of optimists and pessimists have collided forcefully in the debate about the potential contribution of biotechnology and genetic engineering to food security. This technology has been held out as a potential solution to the problem of achieving food security for a growing world population. A careful look at how the optimists and pessimists approach this technology reveals the limitations of each group.

Biotechnologies such as molecular marker-assisted selection or diagnostics are relatively noncontroversial. This is not the case, however, with genetic engineering—the precise modification of hereditary genetic material in living organisms. Genetic engineering allows scientists to insert genes from one species into another unrelated species and produce "transgenic varieties," thereby overcoming natural cross-breeding barriers.

The main objectives of biotechnological research and development for food security are similar to those of conventional breeding:

- secure the given yield potential,

- increase the yield potential, and

- raise productivity.

Efforts to achieve these goals include research for varietal qualities such as resistance to or tolerance of plant diseases (fungi, bacteria, viruses) and animal pests (insects, mites, nematodes) as well as to stress factors such as climatic changes or aridity and poor soil quality. Most scientists and important international institutions explicitly acknowledge the potential of biotechnology and genetic engineering to make a positive contribution in these areas. In its recent *Statement on Biotechnology*, for example, the U.N. Food and Agriculture Organization (FAO) recognized that genetic engineering "has the potential to help increase production and productivity in agriculture, forestry, and fisheries. It could lead to higher yields on marginal lands in countries that today cannot grow enough food to feed their people."[5]

Conventional crop-breeding programs will remain important for the foreseeable future. They have a competitive disadvantage, however, in that they must proceed in small steps toward single targets and are thus time-consuming; in addition, conventional breeding is more limited in scope as it cannot overcome natural cross-breeding barriers. If, in contrast, selection systems are developed that can be implemented in the test tube—through characterization of genetic markers for certain properties, for example—then research can be carried out with much greater efficiency. With the help of biotechnology, it seems likely that apomixis (asexual type of reproduction) for hybrids will be achieved—a potential breakthrough for small and big farmers alike, because they could then take the seed for the next season from their own harvest and would not have to buy it on the market.

In the long term, plants may be developed that can produce vaccines for humans.[6] Edible vaccines delivered in locally grown genetically engineered crops could do more to eliminate disease than the Red Cross, all missionaries, and various U.N. task forces combined—and at a fraction of the cost.[7]

Case studies show that over the past few years biotechnology and—so far, to a lesser extent—genetic engineering have helped to make progress toward food security, be it through resistance to fungal and viral diseases in major food crops or through improved plant properties.[8]

The hope that significant progress can be achieved through the application of genetic engineering and biotechnology for agricultural purposes remains high. A World Bank panel predicts, for example, that efforts to improve rice yields in Asia through biotechnology will result in a production increase of 10–20 percent over the next 10 years.[9] And a recent poll found that German scientists expect genetically engineered drought and salt tolerance to be achieved by 2012 and nitrogen fixation by 2017—which is within the next generation and before world population reaches the 9 billion mark.[10]

All these developments prompted the preparation of a report under the auspices of the Royal Society of London; the national science academies of Brazil, China,

India, Mexico, and the United States; and the Third World Academy of Sciences. Published in July 2000, it noted the following:

- In view of the existing problems and those that can be expected in the future with regard to securing the world's food supply, genetic modification (GM) technology has an important part to play, since it helps to overcome basic problems of resistance that stand in the way of an increase in food production and agricultural productivity.

- The areas in which GM technology is identified as offering potential benefits are pest resistance, improved yield, tolerance to biotic and abiotic stress, use of marginalized land, nutritional benefits, reduced environmental impact, and others.

- It is critical for developing countries to have access to genetic engineering and bitoechnology.[11]

Weighing Benefits and Risks

Despite the benefits promised by genetic engineering and biotechnology, these technologies are no *deus ex machina* for agriculture in developing countries. No technology is of intrinsic value. Humanity has always used and will continue to use technologies as a means to an end. In their decisionmaking processes, societies and individuals have always weighed benefits and risks to arrive at a benefit/risk assessment they can live with.

Are there potential risks associated with this technology? Of course there are—every action (and every non-action) has implicit and explicit risks. No technology in and of itself is good or bad, safe or unsafe, although some are inherently riskier than others, such as live vaccines versus new crop varieties. What makes a technology safe or unsafe is the way it is applied and the outcome of that application. The quantification of any perceived risk can broadly be described as a function of four interrelated variables:

- the scale of the potential harm adjusted by the technology,

- the likelihood of that harm occurring net of use of the technology,

- the ability of an effective response to be put in place adjusted by the technology, and

- the likelihood of that response mechanism being deployed effectively.[12]

Perceived risks must be divided into those that are technology-transcending and those that are inherent to a technology.[13] In the case of technology-inherent risks, a distinction must be drawn between hypothetical and speculative risks. Risks are hypothetical when scientists know they can occur, and how they occur, in the given technological or biological context. Speculative risks are those related to potential, hitherto unknown mechanisms and interactions. Speculative risk assessments are commonly brought forward in a dramatic scenario of assumptions that can be neither scientifically proven nor refuted.

As there is scientific consensus that "the same physical and biological laws govern the response of organisms modified by modern molecular and cellular methods and those produced by classical methods," notes the U.S. National Research Council, and as "no conceptual distinction exists," introducing speculative risks into the debate on transgenic crops is not very helpful.[14]

There is no doubt that agricultural genetic engineering and biotechnology carry serious risks. But in terms of technology-inherent risks (such as allergic reactions in humans, horizontal gene transfer, or the unwanted flow of genes into wild species or landraces), the best of present judgment indicates that genetically modified organisms pose no substantial or unmanageable long-term health hazards for humans or animals.[15] Many unsubstantiated claims continue to circulate, but let the record show the following:

- The sensational report of Pusztai and Even (potatoes transformed with a lectin protein could end up to be poisonous to human health) has been rejected by the vast majority of scientists either because the methodology was flawed or on the grounds that the data do not support the conclusions. (See <http://www.sirc.org/news/pusztai_published.html> and <http://www.freenetpages.co.uk/hp/a.pusztai/>.)

- The old L-tryptophan scare story (eosinophilia-myalgia syndrome caused by the use of a genetically altered *Bacillus amyloliquefaciens*) has been proved wrong.[16]

- Even the much-quoted monarch butterfly laboratory study has been put into empirical perspective. Follow-up studies at Iowa State University and the University of Guelph have indicated that harm to monarchs under field conditions is minimal.[17]

- The risk of allergy to genetically modified foods seems to be controllable and therefore minimal.[18]

In the year 2000, more than 44 million acres around the world were planted with transgenic crops—24 percent of this area being in developing countries.[19] No serious issues—let alone uncontrollable risks—occurred. This record provides empirical support for the conclusion of the U.S. National Academy of Sciences in 1987 that the safety assessment of a recombinant DNA-modified organism should be based on the nature of the organism and the environment into which it will be introduced, not on the method by which it was modified.[20] In addition, on the basis of empirical evidence obtained from studies, the American Medical Association (AMA) concluded at the end of December 2000 that food prepared from genetically modified crops did not pose a risk either for humans or for the environment.[21]

Notwithstanding the high level of safety prevailing at present, this does not mean that the all-clear should be given. Whenever and wherever unresolved questions arise concerning risks of genetically modified food, science-based evaluations should be used on a case-by-case approach to answer them to the best of our ability.[22]

As far as social and political risks are concerned, today's criticism of genetic engineering and biotechnology is structurally similar to discussions about the Green Revolution in the seventies. The improved plant varieties that gave rise to the Green Revolution of the fifties and sixties, particularly in Asia, were developed through systematic selection and crossing (hybridization), with the objective of increasing production and averting famines. Despite undisputed success in achieving significantly higher food production and an overall positive employment effect, there was (and still is) substantial criticism of the Green Revolution as being responsible for growing disparities in poor societies and for the loss of biological diversity.[23] These developments, however, were not a consequence of the technology per se but of the use of the technology in a particular social setting.

Quite apart from this, there are also technology-transcending risks that arise from the yawning gap that opens up between what is scientifically and technically feasible and what is considered to be morally acceptable. Any technology can only be as good as the people who use it.

Normally, the social, economic, and political risks of not using genetic engineering for developing-country agriculture are not part of any technological risk assessments. In view of expected population and natural resource developments over the next 50 years, an approach that tends to overemphasize present perceptions and underestimate the vulnerabilities of future generations presents a great risk to humankind and those future generations. Much of what is dismissed as "not necessary" in the light of present-day conditions would have to be judged differently in a world of 9 billion or more.

A Critical Juncture

Public acceptance of agricultural genetic engineering and biotechnology is at a critical juncture. The next three to five years will be decisive for the long-term viability of this technology. The discussion today in Europe is highly negative and can have a destructive effect on developing countries by reducing support for public research for resource-poor farmers and thus harming their future production conditions and food security. The political economy of agricultural biotechnology could mean that developing countries, which have rapidly growing populations and ever-shrinking natural resources and which depend most on the low-cost availability of this highly effective and productive technology, are denied access to it.

Without doubt the reasons behind the deficits in food security in developing countries are many and complex, and they cannot be overcome by technology. Economic and social policy, principles of equality that create a development-friendly environment for men and women alike, social safety networks, education, credit, and an infrastructure that enables all people to shape their own lives—it is true that a constellation of policies like this is the most important prerequisite for a sustainable solution to the hunger in these countries. But it is no substitute for improved farming methods and the use of state-of-the-art technology. This is a part of the solution, and the world would do well to make use of it and develop it further. The technology and the knowledge are already in place, but a good policy is not. We in the North can afford the luxury of "waiting for Godot," but those in the South do not have that kind of time at their disposal.

Advocating the use of biotechnology and genetic engineering to help improve food security in developing countries is not meant to support these technologies for their own sake or out of context. Biotechnology and genetic engineering should always be seen as part of a wider technological pluralism.[24] Using them is desirable only if and where on a case-by-case basis they have a comparative advantage in solving constraints related to agricultural objectives—that is, if they prove superior to other technologies with regard to cost-effectiveness. Using them appropriately to raise agricultural productivity can gain the world a bit of time to achieve a more sustainable balance between population growth and food supplies.

Ways Out of the Crisis

Over the past 50 years, the scope of the impacts of human activity has grown enor-
mously, in terms of both time and space. Whether we are dealing with medium- or
long-term improvements, time is still of the essence. The following three elements
are essential to a successful, smooth turnaround in ecological trends:

- promotion of ecological innovation and the transfer of such know-how to
  developing countries,

- internalization of environmental costs and consistent application of the pay-as-
  you-pollute principle, and

- promotion of a change in values to support different ideals of modernization
  and environmentally friendly lifestyles.

Promotion of Innovation and Technology Transfer

Innovation is not the only element on the road to sustainable development in industrial and developing countries, but without innovation everything else is to no avail.
The so-called resource efficiency revolution has achieved impressive results.[25] If the
same benefits can be achieved using fewer resources and with less stress on the environment, ecological threats will be less immediate. This will allow time to enhance
the economic and social feasibility of declining birth rates. While loosening ecological constraints is only part of people's obligation as Earth's "leaseholders," its value
should not be underestimated, particularly for economic development in the world's
poorer countries.

Innovation is required in industrial countries in order to achieve the emission
reductions set and jointly adopted at the international climate conventions. At the
same time, innovation is highly important for the transfer of technology to developing countries. The answer to the question of whether India or China or other popu-
lous developing countries would industrialize has long been clear. Now, however, their
industrialization process is primarily based on catching up with an outdated technical and ecological model. If this trend continues, it will negate all the environmental
efforts of industrial countries at a global level. State-of-the-art technology cannot
prevent all additional environmental stress induced by industrialization in the countries of the South, but it can perform a key mitigating function. Hence the transfer
of leading-edge technologies would be in the interest of us all. This key factor for our
global ecological future can be influenced by consistent action.

Substantial capital is needed to develop and transfer new technologies. Here
"capital" is used in the broader sense that covers not only financial, natural, and envi-

ronmental capital, but also human capital. It includes people's abilities and knowledge as well as their collaborative and entrepreneurial skills. Between these different categories of capital there exist relative substitution options—that is, to some extent it may be practical or necessary to reduce one type of capital stock, say raw materials, and use the resources thus gained to increase or improve another capital category, say, human capital. This in turn means that rather than focusing on economic growth per se, industrial countries must strive to create a structure for economic growth that bequeaths to succeeding generations a capital stock—financial, natural, and human resources—that does not restrict their development possibilities or the dimensions and structure of their trading options. If we accept the necessity for technical progress, we must examine the incentives that dictate the direction and speed of technical progress. This brings us to the next key element.

Environmental Costs and the "Polluter Pays" Principle

In democratic societies, top-down reforms are usually limited in impact. Sweeping changes of the kind needed for global sustainable development are seldom made top-down. Rather, they evolve from bottom up into broad social processes.[26] To accelerate this process, it is essential to offer a direct and effective incentive. For most people, the best way is through their wallets. Given prices that "tell the ecological truth," the market could develop major environmental steering power. Internalizing environmental costs—for instance, through emission certificates or carbon taxes—changes relative prices.[27] Environmentally harmful behavior becomes so expensive that it turns environmental protection into a financial incentive; this approach is generally more cost-effective than a government decree or regulation. The price triggers an ecologically desirable structural change in consumption and the production of goods and services. A great deal could already be achieved by discontinuing ecologically counterproductive subsidies.

Since a precise calculation of external costs is not possible, it is necessary to define a "political" price. This process of definition gains social acceptance if it involves as many members of civil society as possible. It is generally agreed that ecologically adjusted prices must be introduced over an extended period gradually, in careful dosages, and on an international scale. Additionally, the process must be tax-neutral—that is, market-driven carbon taxes must not increase the overall tax burden within the economy or sector. Wherever the funds collected from levying carbon taxes (such as those on CO_2 emissions or the sale of environmental certificates) are used to reduce other taxes, the process is referred to as ecological tax reform or tax shifting.[28]

Although some people argue that taking the lead in such environmental initiatives endangers a country's international competitiveness, there is growing evidence that environmental regulations in time enhance the attractiveness of particular locations. One of the most socially attractive variants is to use the potential income from environmental taxes to reduce incidental wage costs or other labor-related production costs. The employee's net salary would remain unchanged. The costs could vary according to economic sector; indexed to the amount of energy used by different industries, this would ensure equitable treatment. It is hoped that these measures would make production not only more ecologically friendly, but also more labor-intensive. This side-effect would be of major value in view of mass unemployment and competition from countries with cheap labor.

As things stand at the present, however, an efficiency revolution driven by market forces will probably be only a staging post on the way to sustainable development. A "sufficiency revolution" must also be achieved—a broadly accepted definition of the quality of life that downplays exclusively material values and de-emphasizes the growth of affluence.[29] The cause must be eliminated in order to avoid the effect. But this presupposes a change in human values.

Alternative Ideals of Modernization and Environmentally Friendly Lifestyles

Many people in the North are alarmed at the rate of population growth in the South and believe that rapid action is required. What they do not know or are unwilling to accept is that since World War II it is not only the global population that has grown at a historically unprecedented rate, but also the consumption of natural resources and hence emissions and the volume of waste. Unless attitudes change significantly, every child born now in the European Community will use over 20 times more natural resources during his or her lifetime than children in most developing countries.

Through the decisions made at the U.N. Conference on Environment and Development in Rio in 1992, the Berlin Conference on Climate in spring 1995, and the Kyoto Conference in 1997, the international community has repeatedly made it clear that a solution to environmental problems necessitates "a change of attitude at the level of the individual and society." Rather than diminishing, however, the negative trends in the global environment have grown more acute.[30] Most experts assume that, given a willingness on the part of everyone involved to take corrective action, emerging problems can be solved and irreversible environmental damage avoided.

A better understanding of the problems must be promoted and environmental awareness raised through increased education on environmental issues and greater exploitation of market forces. Added to this, those who have already grasped the scale of the problem must take more concrete action. Human beings are the perpetrators of global environmental problems, and human beings can avoid future damage through a more caring approach.

This is not the place to discuss models of modernization or make philosophical statements on deceleration, contemporary affluence, the "new minimalism," and the elegance of simplicity. Others have already done so.[31] Unfortunately, while the discourse on new models of affluence is highly attractive from an intellectual standpoint, it seldom has any measurable influence on the concrete day-to-day conduct of its participants. Nevertheless, although asceticism will never find a broad base of willing converts, the "affluence lite" model gives pause for thought.[32]

"Affluence lite" is not a cutback arising from temporary saturation—an increase in the consumption of crackers following repeated opulent gourmet menus. Rather, it is a serious approach that does not necessarily believe that more material consumption means more quality of life. This philosophy is translated into action in a number of ways. Examples include

- letting the train take the strain—using urban commuter transport (although additional investments would need to be made in improving existing services);

- avoiding private transport wherever the destination can be reached on foot or by bicycle (for distances below 3 kilometers or about 2 miles, which account for a good share of the trips by car drivers);

- purchasing local produce in season rather than imported produce;

- consciously seeking ways of pooling durable household goods and means of transport; and

- purchasing items according to the criteria of long life, energy-saving capacity, minimum packaging, reparability, and recycling capability rather than, for instance, attractiveness.

A commitment to this type of social change must come primarily from those who regard themselves as the social elite and, it so happens, are best positioned to reduce consumption without falling into inhospitable forms of existence. Those who regard themselves as the social elite, who conduct their lives accordingly, or who even, with the "discreet charm of the bourgeoisie," impose their demands on society also have an obligation to do more for society as a whole. The widely used term "elite" includes setting a social, economic, and ecological example. Success in this respect depends on impressing on people that although the problems are great, each person's individual contributions can never be too small or unimportant to make a difference. The sum of many individual contributions makes a sizeable contribution; hence everyone should and can make a start by dint of his or her own actions.

Individual contributions to solving global problems are admittedly very small, largely invisible, and in some cases only apparent subsequently to other people or in a completely different place. Not so with sacrifices in terms of personal comfort and mobility: these are immediately obvious and initially looked on negatively. We can all convince ourselves that using the underdeveloped rural public transport service instead of our car in winter or on rainy days will have little or no impact on the future greenhouse effect.[33] Collective amorality has a deadly effect over the long term—of this there is no doubt.

Unless we change our attitude toward "sustainable development," our ideals of modernization for developing countries will be wrongly structured. The example of carbon emissions speaks volumes in this respect: China has now outstripped the United States as the world's largest consumer of coal and is promoting use of this fossil fuel to spur economic development.[34] India, too, is planning to fuel most of its economic development through coal. The consequences of burning such vast quantities of coal are enormous in terms of greenhouse gas emissions. Solutions to protect the atmosphere against such emission volumes are not yet in place. Innovations in process and product technologies in industrial countries, coupled with technology transfers to developing countries, if necessary subsidized by development assistance funds, can push back ecological boundaries. This is now perhaps one of the most important reasons for promoting technical progress and innovation.

The nontransferable lifestyle of the "rich," the distortion of this lifestyle as "the affluent life," and its widespread dissemination to all the corners of the globe by commercial advertising interests exercises a great attraction. Only when we change our thinking of what is "chic" and worth aiming for will we be able to stop our destructive icons of progress from invading the psyche of poor countries. The road from excess to abstinence and an informed simplicity will be steep and rocky. Technical problems have always been easier to resolve than social ones. But awareness is changing.

According to a survey by *The Environmental Monitor* in 1998, while unemployment and job opportunities remain atop the list of people's concerns in the industrial countries, environmental issues have gained substantial ground.[35] Compared with 1992, environmental awareness had increased even in developing countries, primarily in Asia. Local and hence directly discernible environmental problems such as water and air pollution are uppermost, but indirect problems such as climate change or depletion of the ozone layer are a close second. Moreover, the fact that most respondents believed that we should err "on the side of caution"—that is, they would welcome a precautionary approach—is also highly significant.

Changes in attitude and conduct, adequate legal frameworks, and better technologies are the key requirements for a successful reversal of global trends. Yet the need to stabilize world population remains a key goal. If the world population in 2050 matches the lower U.N. projections rather than the medium figures, we could cut down on twice as much carbon dioxide as we could reduce by stopping deforestation. This difference would be equivalent to more than twice the current energy consumption or a 50 percent replacement of current fossil fuel consumption by renewable energy.[36] Population growth plays a major, dynamic role not only in terms of local and regional environmental resources, but also in terms of global environmental burdens.

The Limits of Technology and Substitution

Without a doubt, human knowledge can be substituted to a certain extent for nonrenewable resources. Would people today be better off if they had the natural resources of medieval societies but a medieval level of knowledge? The answer is obvious. Future generations, too, will benefit more from the results of current research and development than from resources left in the ground.

Even if all the world's problems cannot be solved by developing new technologies, it is fair to assume that technical progress will continue to make a significant contribution to solving ecological problems, creating social wealth, and sustaining the "resource efficiency revolution." The time we gain through technical progress is difficult to estimate, but it will facilitate social and ecological adaptation processes, particularly the social and demographic adjustments required of developing countries.

Nevertheless, it would not be wise to rely exclusively on the availability of new technologies. First of all, the extent to which technical progress and human inventiveness can solve problems does not depend merely on new knowledge and capabilities. These advances can make a positive contribution only if the will to improve is present. Technical progress can also bear fruit only under conditions of good governance. Second, by no means can all problems be solved technically. Copper may well be replaceable by carbon fiber for electrical transport, and mobile telephones may well make wires superfluous. From a material point of view it may also be possible to substitute wild fish with fish bred in fish farms, and natural forests with timber farms.

But there is no adequate substitute for the ozone layer, one of our most important collective global commodities. Nor is there any substitute for biological species diversity, one of the cornerstones of life-form systems. Admittedly not every species is worth protecting (consider the malaria-carrying mosquito, the polio pathogen, or HIV), which is why priorities need to be set for biodiversity protection. Since we are still a long way, however, from determining the exact interdependencies between various life forms, we should prevent the extinction of any species wherever possible. And as long as experts continue to disagree on the effects of a higher concentration of greenhouse gases in the atmosphere and the possible consequences of climate change, strategies of response are open to question. This means taking no "unnecessary risks," including unacceptable technical risks. If, however, we have to decide what constitutes "unnecessary" and "necessary" risk, we again confront a problem of values.

The current generation has an opportunity to strengthen the basic moral principles of solidarity and justice, marshal the political commitment necessary to implement these principles, stimulate individual ethical motivation, and mobilize the maximum measure of discipline and commitment possible at all levels of social activity. If we succeed in capitalizing on this opportunity, we could go down in history as the generation that did more than any other to turn humanistic visions into practical results. If we fail, however, we should not expect to be judged kindly by future generations. We will be remembered as the generation that could have charted a course for the better at a relatively small cost but failed to do so out of indifference, indolence, and egotism. In this respect, discussions of population policy and food security are a part of the basic social consensus that must be created.

Will we succeed, in the time we have left, in finding the path to sustainable development with a well-fed population constant in size and with environmentally friendly lifestyles? Or will large sections of the world's population be driven to anarchic conflicts over allocation of resources through absolute scarcity? The answer to this question may lie in an old Chinese parable:

> Three thousand years ago in the province of Chu lived a wise old man who knew the right answer to any question. This annoyed two young men, who set out to play a trick on him and prove that he did not know everything. One of them took a small bird in his hands and hid it behind his back. The other asked the old man: "What is my friend holding behind his back?" The old man answered: "A sweet little bird." Thereupon the young man slyly asked his second question: "And, honorable sage, is the bird alive or dead?" The young men had agreed that if the old man answered that the bird was dead they would release the bird to prove he was wrong. If, however, the old man replied that the bird was alive, the young man would crush the bird and show its corpse to the old man as proof of his fallibility. "Well, old man, is the bird alive or dead?" repeated the young man. The old man smiled and said, "That lies entirely in your own hands."

Notes

Chapter 1, "Six Billion and Counting"

1. Found in D.G. Johnson, "The Growth of Demand Will Limit Output Growth for Food over the Next Quarter Century" (Chicago, IL: Office of Agricultural Economics Research, University of Chicago, 22 August 1998).

2. In addition to "medium" and "high" variants, the United Nations has also calculated a "low" variant of demographic development. It is based on a considerably slower rate of population growth and forecasts a global population of 7.3 billion in 2050. However, since there are great discrepancies between demographic development in reality and the assumptions on which the minimum variant is based, it will be not be considered here.

3. Deutsche Gesellschaft für die Vereinten Nationen, "Aktionsprogramm der Konferenz der Vereinten Nationen über Bevölkerung und Entwicklung (ICPD)," published as *Blaue Reihe Nr. 54*, December 1994.

4. World Health Organization (WHO), *The World Health Report 1998* (Geneva: 1998).

5. Quoted in the summary of United Nations Environment Programme (UNEP), *Global Environment Outlook 1997* (New York: Oxford University Press, 1997), p. 2.

6. See World Bank, *World Development Report 1997* (New York: Oxford University Press, 1997).

7. L.R. Brown, M. Renner, and C. Flavin, *Vital Signs 1998* (New York: Norton, 1998), p. 23.

8. All data, unless otherwise mentioned, are from United Nations Development Programme (UNDP), *Human Development Report 1998* (New York: Oxford University Press, 1998); data for 1999 are from Population Reference Bureau (PRB), *1999 World Population Data Sheet* (Washington, DC: 1999).

9. All data in this section, unless otherwise noted, are from UNDP, op. cit. note 8; data for 1999 are from PRB, op. cit. note 8.

10. WHO, op. cit. note 4, p. v.

11. UNICEF, *The State of the World's Children 1998* (New York: 1998).

12. Data in this section are from UNDP, op. cit. note 8, and from World Bank, *World Development Report 1998* (New York: Oxford University Press, 1998).

13. Incomes of employees and employers diverged by a factor of 4 between 1975 and 1994; in 1975 the ratio was 1:41; in 1994 it was 1:187. This relative deterioration was accompanied by an absolute decline in various industrial countries. Data are from the New York Times, *The Downsizing of America* (New York: Times Books, 1996).

14. See J. Rifkin, "The Fate of Nations," *Social Development Review*, December 1996, p. 8f.

15. World Bank and International Monetary Fund (IMF), *Comprehensive Development Framework* (Washington, DC: 1999), p. 2.

16. UNEP, op. cit. note 5, p. 10.

17. World Resources Institute (WRI) et al., *World Resources 1998–99* (New York: Oxford University Press, 1998), p. 139ff.

18. World Bank, *Advancing Sustainable Development: The World Bank and Agenda 21*, Environmentally Sustainable Development Occasional Papers No. 19 (Washington, DC: 1997), p. 3.

19. Emissions from ibid.; carbon dioxide concentrations from Brown, Renner, and Flavin, op. cit. note 7, p. 66ff.

20. Brown, Renner, and Flavin, op. cit. note 7, p. 68ff. See also L.R. Brown, M. Renner, and B. Halweil, *Vital Signs 1999* (New York: Norton, 1999), p. 58f.

21. WRI et al., op. cit. note 17, p. 140.

22. Brown, Renner, and Flavin, op. cit. note 7, p. 15f.

23. World Bank and IMF, op. cit. note 15, p. 2. See also UNDP, *Human Development Report 1997* (New York: Oxford University Press, 1997), p. 24.

24. WRI et al., op. cit. note 17, p. 140f.

25. Francis Fukuyama, *The End of History and the Last Man* (New York: Free Press, 1992).

26. UNEP, op. cit. note 5, p. 3.

27. United Nations, *World Urbanization Prospects: The 1996 Revision* (New York: 1998), p. 2. All statistics on urbanization are taken from this source unless otherwise indicated.

28. J.L. Garrett, "Overview," in J.L. Garrett and M.T. Ruel (eds.), *Achieving Urban Food and Nutrition Security in the Developing World*, 2020 Focus 3 (Washington, DC: International Food Policy Research Institute [IFPRI], 2000).

29. M. Brockerhoff, "An Urbanizing World," in J.L. Garrett and M.T. Ruel (eds.), *Achieving Urban Food and Nutrition Security in the Developing World*, 2020 Focus 3 (Washington, DC: IFPRI, 2000).

30. Garrett, op. cit. note 28.

31. Ibid.

32. B.M. Popkin, "Urbanization and the Nutrition Transition," in J.L. Garrett and M.T. Ruel (eds.), *Achieving Urban Food and Nutrition Security in the Developing World*, 2020 Focus 3 (Washington, DC: IFPRI, 2000).

33. United Nations Population Fund (UNFPA), *The State of World Population 1998: The New Generations* (New York: 1998).

34. M. Yudelman with L.J.M. Kealy, "The Graying of the World's Population: Implications for Agriculture," unpublished paper prepared for IFPRI, Washington, DC, 1998, p. 2.

35. Ibid., p. 4.

36. Ibid., p. 5.

37. World Health Organization, Geneva, press release, 11 May 1998.

38. A. Barnett and G. Rugalema, "HIV/AIDS," in R. Flores and S. Gillespie (eds.), *Health and Nutrition: Emerging and Reemerging Issues in Developing Countries*, 2020 Focus 5 (Washington, DC: IFPRI, 2001).

39. See Chapter 5 of this book.

40. P.R. Ehrlich and A. Ehrlich, *Betrayal of Science and Reason* (Washington, DC: Island Press, 1996); L.R. Brown, M. Renner, and C. Flavin, *Vital Signs 1999* (New York: Norton, 1999) (published annually for Worldwatch Institute).

41. J.L. Simon, *The State of Humanity* (Oxford: Blackwell, 1995); idem, *The Ultimate Resource 2* (Princeton, NJ: Princeton University Press, 1996); R. Bailey, *The True State of the Planet* (New York: Free Press, 1995).

42. Simon, *The Ultimate Resource 2*, op. cit. note 41.

Chapter 2, "From Population Theory to Reality"

1. United Nations Population Division, *Population Bulletin of the United Nations*, No. 19/20, 1986, p. 36.

2. See United Nations Population Fund (UNFPA), *Population, Resources, and the Environment: The Critical Challenge* (New York: 1991), p. 11.

3. Literally, the "raw birth rate"—the number of children a woman would have if she survived to the end of her childbearing years and bore children according to the prevailing age-specific fertility rates at each point during this period.

4. Defined as a net reproduction rate of 1.

5. N. Keyfitz, "The Limits of Population Forecasting," in K. Davis, M.S. Bernstam, and H.M. Sellers (eds.), *Population and Resources in a Changing World* (Stanford, CA: Morrison Institute for Population and Resource Studies, 1989), p. 77.

6. See C. Haub, "Understanding Population Projections," *Population Bulletin*, vol. 42, no. 4 (1987).

7. See H. Jonas. "Auf der Schwelle der Zukunft: Werte von gestern für eine Welt von morgen," in H. Jonas and D. Mieth, *Was für morgen lebenswichtig ist. Unentdeckte Zukunftswerte* (Freiburg, Germany: Herder, 1983), p. 22ff.

8. Obviously many factors influence the availability of investment capital, such as a country's political situation. See H. de Soto, *The Other Path: The Invisible Revolution in the Third World* (New York: Harper and Row, 1989).

9. T.R. Malthus, *An Essay on the Principle of Population As It Affects the Future Improvement of Society* (London: 1798). In later editions, the title was changed slightly to *An Essay on the Principle of Population or a View on Its Past and Present Effects on Human Happiness* (London: 1893, 1807, 1817, and 1826). The quotation here is from p. 6 of the German edition.

10. Ibid., and p. 9.

11. Ibid., p. 668.

12. Some demographers see a transition consisting of five phases. See C.P. Blacker, "Stages in Population Growth," *Eugenics Review*, vol. 39, no. 3 (1947), pp. 88–101.

13. See F.W. Notestein, "Population—The Long View," in T.W. Schultz (ed.), *Food for the World* (Chicago: University of Chicago Press, 1945), pp. 36–57.

14. A.J. Coale, "The Demographic Transition Reconsidered," in International Union for the Scientific Study of Population (IUSSP), *International Population Conference, 1973*, vol. 1 (Liège, Belgium: 1973), p. 60f. See also P. Demeny, "Early Fertility Decline in Austria-Hungary: A Lesson in Demographic Transition," *Daedalus*, vol. 97, no. 2 (1968), p. 512.

15. For a discussion of why the European model does not apply, see A.J. Coale and S. Cotts Watkins (eds.), *The Decline of Fertility in Europe* (Princeton, NJ: Princeton University Press, 1986), and Coale, op. cit. note 14, p. 56ff.

16. J. Knodel and E. van der Walle, "Lessons from the Past: Policy Implications of Historical Fertility Studies," *Population and Development Review*, vol. 5, no. 2 (1979), pp. 217–45; C.

Hirschmann and P. Guest, "The Emerging Demographic Transition of Southeast Asia," *Population and Development Review*, vol. 16, no. 1 (1990), pp. 121–52.

17. See Y.W. Bradshaw and E.E. Fraser, "City Size, Economic Development, and Quality of Life in China: New Empirical Evidence," *American Sociological Review*, vol. 54 (1989), pp. 986–1003, and idem, "City Size, Birthrates, and Development in China: Evidence of Modernization?"*Journal of Urban Affairs*, vol. 12, no. 4 (1990), pp. 401–24.

18. See T. Bengtsson, "Lessons from the Past: The Demographic Transition Revised," *Ambio*, vol. 21, no. 1 (1992), p. 24f.; N. Keyfitz, "Completing the Worldwide Demographic Transition: The Relevance of Past Experience," *Ambio*, vol. 21, no. 1 (1992), pp. 26–30.

19. L.R. Brown, G. Gardner, and B. Halweil, *Beyond Malthus* (New York: Norton, 1999), p. 118.

20. See, for example, J.L. Simon, *The Ultimate Resource* (Princeton, NJ: Princeton University Press, 1981), and the revised version, *The Ultimate Resource 2* (Princeton, NJ: Princeton University Press, 1996).

21. See Simon, *The Ultimate Resource 2*, op. cit. note 20, and idem, *The State of Humanity* (Oxford: Blackwell, 1995).

Chapter 3, "Social and Economic Impacts of Rapid Population Growth"

1. N. Sadik, "World Population Continues to Rise," *The Futurist*, March–April 1991, p. 9.

2. See the tables on health issues in the United Nations Development Programme's *Human Development Reports* of various years.

3. See Population Reference Bureau (PRB), *Family Planning Saves Lives* (Washington, DC: 1997).

4. See C.E. Taylor, J.S. Newman, and N.U. Kelly, "Interactions between Health and Population," *Studies in Family Planning*, vol. 7, no. 4 (1976); J. Trussell and A.R. Rebley, *The Potential Impact of Changes in Fertility on Infant, Child and Maternal Mortality* (Princeton, NJ: Princeton University Press, 1984); F. Del Mundo, E. Ines-Cuyegkenk, and D. M. Aviado (eds.), *Primary Maternal and Neonatal Health: A Global Concern* (New York: Plenum Press, 1983); and A.R. Omran, "Interrelations between Maternal and Neonatal Health and Family Planning," in ibid., pp. 22–43. See also, for example, J. Cleland and Z. Sathar, "The Effect of Birth Spacing on Childhood Mortality in Pakistan," *Population Studies*, vol. 38, no. 3 (1984), pp. 401–18; and J.N. Hobcraft, J.W. McDonald, and S.O. Rutstein, "Demographic Determinants of Infant and Early Child Mortality: A Comparative Analysis," *Population Studies*, vol. 39, no. 3 (1985), pp. 363–86.

5. Compare D. Maine, R. McNamara, J. Wray, A. Farah, and M. Wallace, "Effects of Fertility Change on Maternal and Child Survival," in G.T.F. Acsadi, G. Johnson-Acsadi, and R.A. Bulatao (eds.), *Population Growth and Reproduction in Sub-Saharan Africa: Technical Analyses of Fertility and Its Consequences* (Washington, DC: World Bank, 1990), pp. 91–114.

6. B. Winikoff and M. Sullivan, "Assessing the Role of Family Planning in Reducing Maternal Mortality," *Studies in Family Planning*, vol. 18, no. 3 (1987), pp. 128–43.

7. See Z. Sathar, "Seeking Explanations for High Levels of Infant Mortality in Pakistan," *Pakistan Development Review*, vol. 26, no. 1 (1987), pp. 55–70.

8. The commonly used expression for this "wasting" is "maternal depletion syndrome," and it naturally depends also on the social circumstances of the woman (for example, income, nutritional condition, and degree of physical labor).

9. The West African word *kwashiorkor*, nowadays a term universally used to describe infant protein-calorie malnutrition, in its literal translation means "disease of the weaned child following the birth of the next child."

10. The tragic situation of an African country is described by A.M. Greenwood, B.M. Greenwood, A.K. Bradley, K. Williams, F.C. Shenton, S. Tulloch, P. Bypass, and F.S.J. Oldfield, "A Prospective Survey of the Outcome of Pregnancy in a Rural Area of The Gambia," *Bulletin of the World Health Organization*, vol. 65, no. 5 (1987), pp. 635–43; see also W. J. Graham, "Maternal Mortality: Levels, Trends, and Data Deficiencies," in R.G. Feachem and D.T. Jamison (eds.), *Disease and Mortality in Sub-Saharan Africa* (Washington, DC: World Bank, 1991), pp. 101–16.

11. See S. Cochrane, V. Kozel, and H. Alderman, *Household Consequences of High Fertility in Pakistan*, World Bank Discussion Paper No. 111 (Washington, DC: 1990), p. 6.

12. PRB, op. cit. note 3.

13. See, for example, M. Selowsky, "The Economic Dimension of Malnutrition in Young Children," in S. Doxiadis (ed.), *The Child in the World of Tomorrow* (Oxford: Oxford University Press, 1979), p. 351.

14. J. Wray and D. Maine, "Family Spacing," in UNICEF, *The State of the World's Children 1984* (New York: Oxford University Press, 1984), p. 94, and the literature mentioned therein.

15. See the Web site of the International Conference on Population and Development (ICPD) (5–13 September 1994), at <www.iisd.ca/linkages/cairo.html>.

16. L. Haddad, C. Pena, C. Nishida, A. Quisumbing, and A. Slack, "Food Security and Nutrition Implications of Intrahousehold Bias: A Review of Literature," Food Consumption and Nutrition Division Discussion Paper 19 (International Food Policy Research Institute [IFPRI], Washington, DC, 1996).

17. N. Birdsall, "A Cost of Siblings: Child Schooling in Urban Colombia," in J. Davanzo and J.L. Simon (eds.), *Research in Population Economics*, vol. 2 (Greenwich, CT: Blackwell, 1980), p. 117.

18. See C. Ernst and J. Angst, *Birth Order: Its Influence on Personality* (New York: Springer, 1983); E.M. King, *Consequences of Population Pressure on the Family's Welfare* (Washington, DC: National Research Council, 1985); G. Rodgers, *Poverty and Population: Approaches and Evidence* (Geneva: International Labour Organisation [ILO], 1984).

19. S.H. Cochrane and D.T. Jamison, "Educational Attainment and Achievement in Rural Thailand," in A.A. Summers (ed.), *Productivity Assessment in Education*, New Directions for Testing and Measurement No. 15 (San Francisco: Jossey-Bass, 1982), pp. 43–59.

20. L.R. Brown, G. Gardner, and B. Halweil, *Beyond Malthus* (New York: Norton, 1999).

21. United Nations Population Fund (UNFPA), *The State of World Population 1991* (New York, 1991).

22. Ibid.

23. All statistical data on age structure can be obtained from the World Bank, *World Development Report 1997* (New York: Oxford University Press, 1997), Table 4, p. 252f.

24. Here, too, this ignores the traditional sector, where children assist in domestic chores and agricultural work from an early age, and, for reasons of poverty, even the elderly usually help until incapacitated or until their death. These statistics relate to the modern sector of the economy, where employment is reimbursed with hard cash.

25. Nevertheless, in the developing world children under 15 and people aged 65 and older contribute in various ways to the family income.

26. See K.M. Leisinger, *Arbeitslosigkeit, Direktinvestitionen und angepasste Technologie* (Berne/Stuttgart: Paul Haput, 1975); also G.M. Farooq and F.L. MacKellar, "Demographic, Employ-

ment and Development Trends: The Need for Integrated Planning," *International Labour Review*, vol. 129, no. 3 (1990), pp. 301–15.

27. See, for example, S. Hansen, "Absorbing a Rapidly Growing Labor Force," in Acsadi, Johnson-Acsadi, and Bulatao, op. cit. note 5, pp. 60–73.

28. See, for example, N.H. Leff, "Dependency Rates and Savings Rates," *American Economic Review*, vol. 59, no. 5 (1969), p. 887f. See also P. Musgrove, "Determinants of Urban Household Consumption in Latin America: A Summary of Evidence from the ECIEL," *Economic Development and Cultural Change*, vol. 26, no. 3 (1978), p. 441ff.; D. Freedman, *Family Size and Economic Welfare in a Developing Country: Taiwan* (Ann Arbor, MI: Population Studies Center, University of Michigan, 1972). For a critical discussion of this subject, see A. Mason, "Saving, Economic Growth, and Demographic Change," *Population and Development Review*, vol. 14, no. 1 (1988), pp. 113–44, and the literature mentioned therein.

29. See A. Coale and E.M. Hoover, *Population Growth and Economic Development in Low-Income Countries* (Princeton, NJ: Princeton University Press, 1958).

30. H. Singer, in UN/E/Conf. 60/SYM 1/36 of the Cairo World Population Symposium, quoted in L. Tabah, *Population Growth and Economic Development in the Third World* (Liège, Belgium: International Union for the Scientific Study of Population [IUSSP], 1975).

31. International Labour Organization, *World Employment Report 1998–99* (Geneva: 1998).

32. Ibid.

33. Brown, Gardner, and Halweil, op. cit. note 20, p. 55.

34. H. Chenery, M.S. Ahluwalia, C.L.G. Bell, J.H. Duloy, and R. Jolly, *Redistribution with Growth*, 3rd ed. (Oxford: Oxford University Press, 1976), p. 17.

35. This view assumes that higher-income earners would exhibit a higher rate of saving. These funds would be deployed for job-creating investments, which in turn would lead in a second period to higher employment and hence rising incomes. See the classic article by R. Barlow, "The Economic Effect of Malaria Eradication," *American Economic Review*, vol. 54 (1967); see also J.E. Meade, "Population Explosion: The Standard of Living and Social Conflict," *Economic Journal*, vol. 77 (June 1967).

36. See I. Hauchler, D. Messner, and F. Nuscheler, *Globale Trends 1998, Fakten, Analysen Prognosen,* Stiftung Entwicklung und Frieden (Frankfurt a.M.: Fischer, 1998), p. 97ff.; see also P. Martin and J. Widgren, "International Migration: A Global Challenge," *Population Bulletin*, vol. 51, no. 1 (1996).

37. Hauchler, Messner, and Nuscheler, op. cit. note 36.

Chapter 4, "Pressures on Natural Systems"

1. For a comprehensive introduction to the subject of water, see P.H. Gleick, *The World's Water: The Biennial Report on Freshwater Resources* (Washington, DC: Island Press, 1998).

2. R.S. Meinzen-Dick and M.W. Rosegrant, "Overview," *Overcoming Water Scarcity and Quality Constraints*, 2020 Focus 9, Brief 1 (Washington, DC: IFPRI, 2001).

3. See J.C. Glenn and T.J. Gordon, *State of the Future: Issues and Opportunities* (Washington, DC: American Council for the United Nations University, 1998).

4. World Health Organization (WHO), *The World Health Report 1998* (Geneva: 1998).

5. World Meteorological Organization, *Comprehensive Assessment of the Freshwater Resources of the World* (New York: 1997).

6. Ibid. Other sources assume a 10-fold increase; see I. Serageldin, "Managing Water Resources Sustainably: Challenges and Solutions for the New Millennium," in *Revue Internationale de l'Eau,* no. 2 (1998).

7. M.W. Rosegrant, C. Ringler, and R.V. Gerpacio, "Water and Land Resources and Global Food Supply," paper prepared for 23rd International Conference of Agricultural Economists, Sacramento, CA, 10–16 August 1997.

8. P. Pinstrup-Andersen, R. Pandya-Lorch, and M.W. Rosegrant, *The World Food Situation: Recent Developments, Emerging Issues, and Long-Term Prospects,* Food Policy Report (Washington, DC: IFPRI, 1997), pp. 23–24.

9. M. Rosegrant and X. Cai, "Water for Food Production," in *Overcoming Water Scarcity and Quality Constraints,* 2020 Focus 9, ed. R. Meinzen-Dick and M. Rosegrant (Washington, DC: IFPRI, 2001).

10. R. Engelman and P. LeRoy, *Sustaining Water: Population and the Future of Renewable Water Supplies* (Washington, DC: Population and Environment Program, Population Action International, 1993).

11. S. Postel, *Last Oasis* (New York: Norton, 1992), p. 20.

12. U.N. Food and Agriculture Organization (FAO), *FAOSTAT Database,* electronic database, <apps.fao.org>.

13. Pinstrup-Andersen, Pandya-Lorch, and Rosegrant, op. cit. note 8, p. 24.

14. FAO, *World Food Summit Technical Background Documents,* vol. 1 (Rome: 1996), p. 26ff.

15. "Water and Food Security," in ibid.

16. S. Postel, "Water for Food Production: Will There Be Enough in 2025?" *BioScience,* vol. 48, no. 8 (1998), pp. 629–37.

17. See, for example, ibid., and S. Postel, *Pillar of Sand* (New York: Norton, 1999), p. 164ff.

18. D. Seckler, *The New Era of Water Resource Management: From "Dry" to "Wet" Water Savings* (Washington, DC, and Colombo, Sri Lanka: Consultative Group on International Agricultural Resources and International Water Management Institute, 1996).

19. D. Seckler, U. Amarasinghe, D. Molden, R. de Silva, and R. Barker, *World Water Demand and Supply, 1990–2025: Scenarios and Issues,* Research Report No. 19 (Colombo, Sri Lanka: International Water Management Institute [IWMI], 1998), p. 13f. See also Organisation for Economic Co-operation and Development (OECD), *Water Consumption and Sustainable Water Resource Management* (Paris, 1998), p. 21.

20. World Resources Institute (WRI), United Nations Development Programme (UNDP), United Nations Environment Programme (UNEP), and World Bank, *World Resources 1998–99* (New York: Oxford University Press, 1998).

21. See A. Wieder, "Coping with Water Deficiency in Arid and Semi-Arid Countries through High-Efficiency Water Management,"*Ambio,* vol. 6, no. 1 (1977), pp. 77–82.

22. M. Rosegrant, "Dealing with Water Scarcity in the Next Century," 2020 Brief 21 (Washington, DC: IFPRI, 1995).

23. See J. Kalbermatten, "Should We Pay for Water? And If So, How?"*Urban Age,* vol. 6, no. 3 (1999), p. 14f.

24. See also Organisation for Economic Co-operation and Development (OECD), *Water Consumption and Sustainable Water Resource Management* (Paris, 1998), p. 79.

25. German Advisory Council on Global Change, *World in Transition: Ways toward Sustainable Management of Freshwater Resources* (Berlin: Springer, 1997).

26. See, for example, S.M.A. Salman and L. Boisson de Chazournes (eds.), *International Watercourses: Enhancing Cooperation and Managing Conflict,* Proceedings of a World Bank Seminar (Washington, DC: 1998), and the literature referred to therein.

27. Rosegrant, op. cit. note 22.

28. FAO, op. cit. note 14.

29. WRI et al., op. cit. note 20, p. 280.

30. S.J. Scherr, "Soil Degradation: A Threat to Developing-Country Food Security by 2020?" 2020 Brief 58 (Washington, DC: IFPRI, 1999).

31. Ibid.

32. The statistics vary depending on the source; we have drawn on Scherr, op. cit. note 30, p. 21.

33. Scherr, op. cit. note 30.

34. Compare A. Chisholm and R. Dumsday (eds.), *Land Degradation: Policies and Problems* (New York: Cambridge University Press, 1987); see also M.K. Tolba, "Our Biological Heritage under Siege," *BioScience,* vol. 39 (1986), p. 725 ff.

35. United Nations Population Fund (UNFPA), *The State of World Population 1990* (New York: 1990).

36. D.V.V. Narayana and B. Ram, "Estimation of Soil Erosion in India," *Journal of Irrigation and Drainage Engineering,* vol. 109, no. 4 (1983), quoted in B. Messerli et al., *Umweltprobleme und Entwicklungszusammenarbeit* (Berne: University of Berne Institute of Geography, 1989), p. 13.

37. S. Dondeyne, K. Opoku-Ameyow, O. Puginier, and C. Sumarde, "Agricultural Land-use in Eroding Uplands: A Case Study in the Philippines," *Tropicultura,* vol. 13, no. 1 (1993), pp. 25–31.

38. See A. Crump, *Dictionary of Environment and Development: People, Places, Ideas and Organizations* (London: Earthscan, 1991), p. 31.

39. Scherr, op. cit. note 30, p. 28.

40. Represented by the case of Ethiopia: H. Hurni, "Land Degradation, Famine, and Land Resource Scenarios in Ethiopia," in D. Pimentel (ed.), *World Soil Erosion and Conservation.* (Cambridge: Cambdridge University Press, 1993), pp. 27–61.

41. Scherr, op. cit. note 30.

42. See G.V. Jacks and R.O. Whyte, *The Rape of the Earth: A World Survey of Soil Erosion* (London: Faber & Faber, 1939).

43. Scherr, op. cit. note 30, p. 31f.

44. B.G. Rozanov, V. Targulian, and D.S. Orlov, "Soils," in B.L. Turner, J.F. Richards, and W.B. Meyer (eds.), *The Earth as Transformed by Human Action* (Cambridge: Cambridge University Press, 1990).

45. C. Rosenzweig and D. Hillel, *Climate Change and the Global Harvest* (New York: Oxford University Press, 1998).

46. Messerli et al., op. cit. note 36, p. 16.

47. See M. Tiffen, M. Mortimore, and F. Gichuki, *More People, Less Erosion: Environmental Recovery in Kenya* (London: Overseas Development Institute, 1994).

48. See S.R. Templeton and S.J. Scherr, "Population Presssure and the Microeconomy of Land Management in Hills and Mountains of Developing Countries," Environment and Production Technology Division Discussion Paper No. 26 (IFPRI, Washington, DC, 1997), p. 5f.

49. See P. Blaikie and H. Brookfield (eds.), *Land Degradation and Society* (New York: Methuen, 1987).

50. Scherr, op. cit. note 30.

51. For a case study, see G. Zelecke and H. Hurni, *Land Use/Land Cover Dynamics and Their Implications for Mountain Resource Degradation in the North-western Ethiopian Highlands* (Bern: University of Bern, Institute of Geography, Centre for Development and Environment, 1999).

52. G. Hardin, "The Tragedy of the Commons," in M.D. Bayles (ed.), *Ethics and Population* (Cambridge, MA: Schenkman, 1976), pp. 3–18; see also D. Wacher, *Land Tenure and Sustainable Management of Agricultural Soils* (Berne: Centre for Development and Environment, Institute of Geography, University of Berne, 1996).

53. Templeton and Scherr, op. cit. note 48.

54. "Forests" naturally refers to all the forests of the world. However, the ongoing problems of dying forests in industrial countries are not discussed here, despite their major importance for some areas (such as Siberia). For an introduction to the subject of tropical rain forests, see T.C. Whitmore, *An Introduction to Tropical Rain Forests* (Oxford: Clarendon Press, 1990).

55. Norman Myers argues that the protection of forests will only be accorded the requisite priority in resource allocation when their profusion and value to humankind is acknowledged and understood. Until then, however, help often arrives too late. See N. Myers, "The World's Forests: Problems and Potentials," *Environmental Conservation,* vol. 23, no. 2 (1996), pp. 156–168; for a quantification of forests' benefits, see ibid., p. 164f.

56. FAO, *The State of the World's Forests 1999* (Rome: 1999), Part I.

57. G.O. Barney et al., *The Global 2000 Report to the President* (New York: Pergamon, 1980).

58. J.N. Abramovitz, "Sustaining the World's Forests," in L.R. Brown et al., *State of the World 1998* (New York: Norton, 1998), p. 23.

59. See German Parliamentary Enquiry Commission "Vorsorge zum Schutz der Erdatmosphäre" (ed.), *Schutz der Tropenwälder. Eine internationale Schwerpunktaufgabe* (Bonn: Economica, 1990), Vol. 2, particularly Section G, pp. 239–70; see also A.K. Saxena, J.C. Nautiyal, and D.K. Foot, "Understanding the Role of Population in Deforestation," *Journal of Sustainable Forestry,* vol. 7, no. 1/2 (1998), pp. 57–110, and A.M. Mannion, *Global Environmental Change: A Natural and Cultural Environmental History* (London: Longman, 1991), p. 237f., 239, and 241ff.

60. German Parliamentary Enquiry Commission, op. cit. note 59, p. 239.

61. UNFPA, *Population, Resources and the Environment: The Critical Challenges* (New York: 1991), p. 44.

62. Carbon emissions from S. Postel and J.C. Ryan, "Reforming Forestry," in L.R. Brown et al., *State of the World 1991* (New York: Norton, 1991); for others, see U.N. Environment Programme, *The State of the Global Environment 1972–1992: Saving our Planet: Challenges and Hopes* (Nairobi: 1992), pp. 49–50.

63. Mannion, op. cit. note 59, p. 153f.

64. See Abramovitz, op. cit. note 58, pp. 35–40.

65. For details, see FAO, op. cit. note 56.

66. For an introduction to this complex problem, see P.R. Ehrlich, "The Loss of Biodiversity: Causes and Consequences," in E.O. Wilson (ed.), *Biodiversity* (Washington, DC: National Academy Press, 1988), p. 21ff.; see also C. Folke, K.-G. Maler, and C. Perrings (eds.), "Special Issue: Economics of Biodiversity Loss," *Ambio,* vol. 21, no. 3 (1992).

67. See I. Hauchler, D. Messner, and F. Nuscheler, *Globale Trends 1998: Fakten, Analysen Prognosen,* Stiftung Entwicklung und Frieden (ed.) (Frankfurt a.M.: Fischer, 1998), p. 267.

68. BirdLife International, *Putting Biodiversity on the Map: Priority Areas for Global Conservation* (Cambridge, UK: International Council for Bird Preservation, 1992).

69. Messerli et al., op. cit. note 36, p. 21.

70. German Parliamentary Enquiry Commission, op. cit. note 59, p. 495.

71. See Hauchler, Messner, and Nuscheler, op. cit. note 67, p. 269.

72. J.H. Connell, "Diversity in Tropical Rain Forests and Coral Reefs," *Science,* vol. 199 (1978), pp. 1302–10.

73. While species extinction has always been an integral part of evolution, the speed and extent have risen dramatically through forest destruction, increased environmental stress, and other changes in the habitats of threatened species. Whereas it is estimated that one species per century died out in prehistoric times, by the beginning of the twentieth century this had increased to one species per year. Now the loss is estimated to be up to 10 species a day. See H. Bossel, *Umweltwissen. Daten, Fakten, Zusammenhänge* (Berlin: Springer, 1990), p. 98.

Chapter 5, "Assuring Food Security for a Growing Population"

1. M.W. Rosegrant, M.S. Paisner, S. Meijer, and J. Witcover, *Global Food Projections to 2020: Emerging Trends and Alternative Futures* (Washington, DC: International Food Policy Research Institute [IFPRI], 2001).

2. World Bank, *Poverty and Hunger,* Policy Study (Washington, DC: 1986).

3. See World Health Organization (WHO), *Nutrition for Health and Development: Progress and Prospects on the Eve of the 21st Century* (Geneva: 1999); U.N. Administrative Committee on Coordination/ Sub-Committee on Nutrition (ACC/SCN), *Fourth Report on the World Nutrition Situation* (Geneva: ACC/SCN in collaboration with IFPRI, 2000).

4. D.E. Sahn and J. von Braun, "The Implications of Variability in Food Production for National and Household Food Security," in J.R. Anderson and P.B.R. Hazell (eds.), *Variability in Grain Yields* (Baltimore, MD: Johns Hopkins University Press for IFPRI, 1989), pp. 320–38.

5. P.B.R. Hazell, "Changing Patterns of Variability in World Cereal Production," in Anderson and Hazell, op. cit. note 4, pp. 13–34.

6. D.E. Sahn (ed.), *Seasonal Variability in Third World Agriculture: The Consequences for Food Security* (Baltimore, MD: Johns Hopkins University Press for IFPRI, 1989); R. Chambers, R. Longhurst, and A. Pacey (eds.), *Seasonal Dimensions to Rural Poverty* (London: Frances Pinter, 1981).

7. See the excellent United Nations Development Programme (UNDP), *Human Development Report 1997* (New York: 1997).

8. R. McNamara, *Address to the Board of Governors,* Nairobi, 24 September 1973.

9. World Bank and International Monetary Fund (IMF), *Comprehensive Development Framework* (Washington, DC: 1999).

10. The economic factors include a high inflation rate, unrealistic exchange rates, the structure of government edicts, commodity prices, terms of trade, or real interest rates. Examples of social factors are lack of education and training or lack of property, while ecological factors include declining soil fertility, as discussed extensively earlier.

11. United Nations, *The World's Women: Trends and Statistics 1970–1990* (New York: 1991).

12. See J. Drèze and A. Sen (eds.), *The Political Economy of Hunger,* 3 vols. (Oxford: Clarendon Press, 1993); A. Sen, *Poverty and Famines: An Essay on Entitlement and Deprivation* (Oxford: Oxford University Press, 1981); and World Institute for Development Economics Research, *Hunger and Entitlements: Research for Action* (Helsinki: 1987).

13. See U. Oltersdorf and L. Weingärtner (eds.), *Handbuch der Welternährung. Die zwei Gesichter der globalen Nahrungssituation* (Bonn: J.H.W. Dietz, 1996), p. 13.

14. J. Becker, *Hungry Ghosts: Mao's Secret Famine* (New York: Free Press, 1997).

15. The statistics vary widely. Detailed studies show much lower figures with respect to hunger-related deaths. See J. Seaman, "Famine Mortality in Ethiopia and Sudan," in E. van der Walle, G. Pison, and M. Sala-Diakanda (eds.), *Mortality and Society in Sub-Saharan Africa* (Oxford: Clarendon Press, 1992), pp. 349–66; J.C. Caldwell and P. Caldwell, "Famine in Africa: A Global Perspective," in ibid., pp. 367–90.

16. E. Messer, M.J. Cohen, and J. D'Costa, *Food from Peace: Breaking the Links between Conflict and Hunger*, 2020 Discussion Paper 24 (Washington, DC: IFPRI, 1998).

17. U.N. Food and Agriculture Organization (FAO), *Food Crops and Shortages* (Rome: 2001).

18. Messer, Cohen, and D'Costa, op. cit. note 16.

19. FAO, *Foodcrops and Shortages: Global Information and Early Warning System on Food and Agriculture* (Rome: 1999).

20. J. von Braun, T. Teklu, and P. Webb, *Famine in Africa: Causes, Responses, and Prevention* (Baltimore, MD: Johns Hopkins University Press for IFPRI, 1998).

21. E. Pollitt, *Malnutrition and Infection in the Classroom* (Paris: U.N. Economic, Social, and Cultural Organization [UNESCO], 1990).

22. H.J. Leonard et al., *Environment and the Poor: Development Strategies for a Common Agenda* (New Brunswick, NJ: Transaction Books for the Overseas Development Council, 1989).

23. The dependency ratio is the proportion of persons of working age relative to the proportion of child dependents and old-age dependents. A high dependency ratio means that each working-age person must support a larger number of people.

24. J. von Braun and R. Pandya-Lorch, "Income Sources of Malnourished People in Rural Areas: A Synthesis of Case Studies and Implications for Policy," in J. von Braun and R. Pandya-Lorch (eds.), *Income Sources of Malnourished People in Rural Areas: Microlevel Information and Policy Implications*, Working Papers on Commercialization of Agriculture and Nutrition No. 5 (Washington, DC: IFPRI, 1991).

25. L.J. Haddad, J. Sullivan, and E. Kennedy, "Identification and Evaluation of Alternative Indicators of Food and Nutrition Security: Some Conceptual Issues and an Analysis of Extant Data" (IFPRI, Washington, DC, 1991, mimeo).

26. J. Pender and P. Hazell, "Overview," in J. Pender and P. Hazell (eds.), *Promoting Sustainable Development in Less-Favored Areas*, 2020 Focus 4 (Washington, DC: IFPRI, 2000).

27. See FAO, *Production Yearbook* (Rome: various years), and <www.fao.org>.

28. L.R. Brown, "Feeding Nine Billion," in L.R. Brown et al., *State of the World 1999* (New York: Norton, 1999), p. 115ff.

29. See, for example, S. Amin, *Die ungleiche Entwicklung* (Hamburg: Hoffmann and Campe, 1975).

30. See, for example, Lord P.T. Bauer, *Equality, the Third World, and Economic Delusion*, 2nd ed. (Cambridge, MA: Harvard University Press, 1982).

31. Quote from R. Behrendt, "Die Zukunft der Entwicklungsländer als Problem des Spät-marxismus," in M. Bohnet (ed.), *Das Nord-Süd Problem* (Munich: 1991), p. 94; B. Davidson, *The Black Man's Burden: Africa and the Curse of the Nation-State* (New York: Times Books, 1992).

32. J.K. Galbraith, *The Affluent Society* (Boston: Houghton Mifflin, 1958).

33. Y.K. Museveni, *What Is Africa's Problem?* (Kampala: NRM Publications, 1992), Chapters 9 and 17.

34. O. Badiane and C.L. Delgado, *A 2020 Vision for Food, Agriculture, and the Environment in Sub-Saharan Africa*, 2020 Discussion Paper 4 (Washington, DC: IFPRI, 1995), p. 3.

35. G. Gardner, "Grain Area Shrinks Again," in L.R. Brown, M. Renner, and B. Halweil, *Vital Signs 2000* (New York: Norton, 2000), p. 45.

36. FAO, *FAOSTAT Database*, electronic database, <apps.fao.org>.

37. "Phenomenal Increase in Maize Production in West and Central Africa," *CGIAR News* (Consultative Group on International Agricultural Research, Washington, DC), vol. 4, no. 2 (1997), pp. 1, 14, 15.

38. United Nations, *World Population Prospects: The 1996 Revisions* (New York: 1996).

39. IMPACT is a global food model covering 37 countries and country groups and 18 major agricultural commodities. The base data are averages of the 1994–96 FAO annual data. The model has been developed and is periodically updated by M.W. Rosegrant and his colleagues at IFPRI. This section draws extensively from several publications that present results of the model: M.W. Rosegrant et al., op. cit. note 1; M.W. Rosegrant, M.S. Paisner, S. Meijer, and J. Witcover, *2020 Global Food Outlook: Trends, Alternatives, and Choices*, Food Policy Report (Washington, DC: IFPRI, 2001); and P. Pinstrup-Andersen, R. Pandya-Lorch, and M.W. Rosegrant, *World Food Prospects: Critical Issues for the Early 21st Century*, Food Policy Report (Washington, DC: IFPRI, 1999).

40. C. Delgado, M. Rosegrant, H. Steinfeld, S. Ehui, and C. Courbois, *Livestock to 2020: The Next Food Revolution*, 2020 Discussion Paper 28 (Washington, DC: IFPRI, 1999).

41. See P. Pinstrup-Andersen, R.Pandya-Lorch, and M.W. Rosegrant, "Food Security: Problems, Prospects, and Policies" (IFPRI, Washington, DC, 2000, mimeo).

42. Ibid.

43. A.F. McCalla and C.L. Revoredo, *Prospects for Global Food Security: A Critical Appraisal of Past Projections and Predictions*, 2020 Brief 71 (Washington, DC: IFPRI, 2001).

Chapter 6, "Population and Sociocultural Norms in Traditional Societies"

1. See B. Musembi and D.E. Anderson, *Religious Communities and Population Concerns* (Washington, DC: Population Reference Bureau, 1994). See also E.A. Hammel, "A Theory of Culture for Demography," *Population and Development Review*, vol. 16, no. 3 (1990), pp. 455–85, and the literature referred to therein.

2. See J. Simons, "Culture, Economy and Reproduction in Contemporary Europe," in D. Coleman and R. Schofield, *The State of Population Theory: Forward from Malthus* (Oxford: Basil Blackwell, 1986), pp. 256–78.

3. See K. Davis, "Institutional Patterns Favoring High Fertility in Underdeveloped Areas," *Eugenics Quarterly*, vol. 2, no. 1 (1955), p. 33ff. See also H. Leridon and B. Ferry, "Biological and Traditional Restraints on Fertility," in J. Cleland and J. Hobcraft (eds.), *Reproductive Change in Developing Countries: Insights from the World Fertility Survey* (Oxford: Oxford University Press, 1985), pp. 139–64.

4. See C. Oppong, "Some Aspects of Anthropological Contributions," in G.M. Farooq and G.B. Simmons, *Fertility in Developing Countries: An Economic Perspective on Research and Policy Issues* (New York: MacMillan, 1985), p. 240ff.

5. See B.A. Shaw, "Fertility and Child Spacing among the Urban Poor in a Third World City: The Case of Calcutta, India," *Human Ecology*, vol. 16, no. 3 (1988), pp. 329–42.

6. See, for example, J. Caldwell and P. Caldwell, "Cultural Forces Tending to Sustain High Fertility," in G.T.F. Acsadi, G. Johnson-Acsadi, and R.A. Bulatao (eds.), *Population Growth and Reproduction in Sub-Saharan Africa: Technical Analysis of Fertility and Its Consequences* (Washington, DC: World Bank, 1990), p. 199, and the literature mentioned therein, especially P.A. Talbot, *Some Niger-*

ian Fertility Cults (London: Oxford University Press, 1927), and J.S. Mbiti, *Concepts of God in Africa* (New York: Praeger, 1970).

7. See also P.N. Hess, *Population Growth and Socio-Economic Progress in Less Developed Countries: Determinants of Fertility* (New York/London: Praeger, 1988), chapters 5 and 6.

8. See D.P. Warwick, "The Indonesian Family Planning Program: Government Influence and Client Choice," *Population and Development Review*, vol. 12, no. 3 (1986), pp. 453–90.

9. For a general discussion of demography in Islamic nations, see J.R. Weeks, "The Demography of Islamic Nations," *Population Bulletin*, vol. 43, no. 4 (1988).

10. See T.H. Hull, "Cultural Influences on Fertility Decision Styles," in R.A. Bulatao and R.D. Lee (eds.), *Determinants of Fertility in Developing Countries, Vol. 2: Fertility Regulation and Institutional Influences* (New York: Academic Press, 1983), pp. 381–414; I. Schapera, *Married Life in an African Tribe* (Middlesex, U.K.: Pelican, 1940); K.M. Whyte, "Cross-cultural Codes Dealing with the Relative Status of Women," in H. Barry and A. Schlegel (eds.), *Cross-cultural Samples and Codes* (Pittsburgh, PA: University of Pittsburgh Press, 1980), pp. 335–61; and L.J. Beckman, "Couples' Decision-Making Processes Regarding Fertility," in K.E. Taeuber, L.L. Bumpass, and J.A. Sweet (eds.), *Social Demography* (New York: Academic Press, 1978), pp. 209–31.

11. See P.E. Hollerbach, "Power in Families: Communication and Fertility Decision-Making," *Journal of Population*, vol. 3, no. 2 (1980).

12. See G. Hartfiel and K.-H. Hillmann, *Wörterbuch der Soziologie*, 3rd ed. (Stuttgart: Kröner, 1982), p. 575.

13. J.C. Caldwell, "Toward a Restatement of Demographic Transition Theory," *Population and Development Review*, vol. 2, no. 3/4 (1976), p. 340.

14. See, for example, G.T. Acsadi and G. Johnson-Acsadi, *Demand for Children and Spacing in Sub-Saharan Africa*, PHN Technical Note No. 85-6 (Washington, DC: World Bank, 1985).

15. J.C. Caldwell, "A Theory of Fertility: From High Plateau to Destabilization," *Population and Development Review*, vol. 4, no. 4 (1978), p. 568.

16. See N.E. Riley, "Gender, Power, and Population Change," *Population Bulletin*, vol. 52, no. 1 (1997), and J. Lorber, *Paradoxes of Gender* (New Haven, CT: Yale University Press, 1994).

17. Population Reference Bureau, *Women of Our World 1998* (Washington, DC: 1998).

18. United Nations, *The World's Women 1970–1990: Trends and Statistics* (New York: 1991).

19. United Nations Population Fund (UNFPA), *The State of World Population 1997: The Right to Choose* (New York: 1997), and the literature mentioned therein.

20. The history of infanticide—especially of female infanticide—is a long one. See J. Lee and W. Feng, "Malthusian Models and Chinese Realities: The Chinese Demographic System 1700–2000," *Population and Development Review*, vol. 25, no. 1 (1999), pp. 33–65; M. das Gupta, "Selective Discrimination against Female Children in India," *Population and Development Review*, vol. 13, no. 1 (1987), pp. 77–101; P.K. Muhuri and S.H. Preston, "Effects of Family Composition on Mortality Differentials by Sex among Children in Matlab, Bangladesh," *Population and Development Review*, vol. 17, no. 3 (1991), pp. 415–34; A. Haupt, "The Shadow of Female Infanticide," *Intercom*, vol. 11, no. 1/2 (1983), pp. 13–14; and T.H. Hull, "Recent Trends in Sex Ratios at Birth in China," *Population and Development Review*, vol. 16, no. 1 (1990), pp. 63–83. No problems of this kind were found in Africa south of the Sahara; see K. Gbenyon and T. Locoh, "Morality Differences in Childhood by Sex in Sub-Saharan Africa," in E. van der Walle, G. Pison, and M. Sala-Diakanda (eds.), *Mortality and Society in Sub-Saharan Africa* (Oxford: Clarendon Press, 1992), pp. 230–52.

21. UNFPA, *The State of World Population 1989* (New York: 1989).

22. M.E. Khan, I. Khan, and N. Mukerjee, "Males' Attitude toward Sexuality and Their Sexual Behaviour: Observations from Rural Gujarat," at <www.popcouncil.org/gfd/partnership3.html>.

23. <http://www.iisd.ca/linkages/Cairo/program/p07008.html>.

24. See J.C. Caldwell, "Mass Education as a Determinant of the Timing of Fertility Decline," *Population and Development Review*, vol. 6, no. 2 (1980); see also United Nations Population Division, *Relationships between Fertility and Education* (New York: 1983), and S.H. Cochrane, *Fertility and Education: What Do We Really Know?* World Bank Staff Occasional Papers No. 26 (Baltimore, MD: Johns Hopkins University Press, 1979).

25. S. Singh and J. Casterline, "The Socio-Economic Determinants of Fertility," in Cleland and Hobcraft, op. cit. note 3, p. 204f.

26. S.H. Cochrane, "Effects of Education and Urbanization on Fertility," in Bulatao and Lee, op. cit. note 10, p. 613.

27. Hess, op. cit. note 7, p. 64f. and p. 133.

28. A.I. Hermalin, "Fertility Regulation and Its Costs: A Critical Essay," in Bulatao and Lee, op. cit. note 10, p. 16f.; see also G.M. Farooq, "Household Fertility Decision-Making in Nigeria," in Farooq and Simmons, op. cit. note 4, p. 341f.; M.T.R. Sarma, "Demand for Children in Rural India," in ibid., pp. 351–64; S. Singh and J. Casterline, "The Socio-Economic Determinants of Fertility," in Cleland and Hobcraft, op. cit. note 3, p. 205.

29. Cochrane, op. cit. note 26; see also J. Cleland and G. Rodriguez, "The Effect of Parental Education on Marital Fertility in Developing Countries," *Population Studies*, vol. 42, no. 3 (1988), pp. 419–42.

30. Singh and Casterline, op. cit. note 28, p. 199ff.

31. S. Saure, "Frauenbildung," in C. Donner-Reichle and L. Klemp (eds.), *Frauenwort für Menschenrechte. Sozialwissenschaftliche Studien zu internationalen Problemen Bd. 46* (Saarbrücken: Breitenbach Verlag, 1990), p. 225ff.

32. United Nations, op. cit. note 18.

33. S.H. Cochrane, D.J. O'Hara, and J. Leslie, *The Effects of Education on Health,* World Bank Staff Working Paper No. 405 (Washington, DC: 1980); R.R. Puffer and C. Serrano, *Patterns of Mortality in Childhood* (Washington, DC: Pan American Health Organization, 1973), pp. 285–94; Cochrane, op. cit. note 26, p. 94ff.; J.C. Caldwell, "Education as a Factor of Mortality Decline: An Examination of Nigerian Data," *Population Studies*, vol. 33, no. 3 (1979), pp. 395–413; UNICEF, *The State of the World's Children 1999* (New York: Oxford University Press, 1999).

34. L.C. Smith and L. Haddad, "Overcoming Child Malnutrition in Developing Countries: Past Achievements and Future Choices," 2020 Brief 64 (Washington, DC: International Food Policy Research Institute [IFPRI], February 2000).

35. Ibid.

36. Ibid.

37. See C.B. Lloyd, "Understanding the Relationship between Women's Work and Fertility: The Contribution of the World Fertility Surveys," Research Division Working Papers No. 9 (New York: Population Council, 1990).

38. UNFPA, *Weltbevölkerungsbericht 1992* (Bonn: 1992), p. 17.

39. E.G.E. Kennedy and L. Haddad, "Food Security and Nutrition 1971–1991: Lessons Learned and Future Priorities," *Food Policy*, vol. 17, no. 1 (1992), p. 2–6; see also M. Garcia, "Impact of Female Sources of Income on Food Demand among Rural Households in the Philippines," *Quarterly Journal of International Agriculture*, vol. 30, no. 2 (1991), p. 109–24.

40. M. Carr, "Technologies for Rural Women: Impact and Dissemination," in A. Iftikhar (ed.), *Technology and Rural Women: Conceptual and Empirical Issues* (London: George Allen and Unwin, 1985).

41. R.L. Blumberg, "Gender Matters: Involving Women in Development in Latin America and the Caribbean," prepared for the U.S. Agency for International Development Bureau for Latin America and the Caribbean (Washington, DC: 1990).

42. A.R. Quisumbing and R.S. Meinzen-Dick, "Overview," *Empowering Women to Achieve Food Security,* 2020 Focus 6 (Washington, DC: IFPRI, 2001).

43. A.R. Quisumbing, L.R. Brown, H.S. Feldstein, L. Haddad, and C. Pena, "Women: The Key to Food Security," Food Policy Statement No. 21 (Washington, DC: IFPRI, 1995).

44. Ibid.

45. Ibid.

46. See, for example, M. Cain, *Women's Status and Fertility in Developing Countries: Preference and Economic Security,* Population and Development Series No. 7 (Washington, DC: World Bank, 1984).

47. For a developing world view on this, see S. Jayasuriya and D.C. Jayasuriya, *Women and Development: The Road from Beijing* (New Delhi: Har-Anand, 1999).

48. This does not mean that there are no latent views of what constitutes "enough children." The average number of children desired decreases as the number of children already born and living increases. In a study of 13 African countries, the number of children per family projected from the number desired by families varied between 6 (Lesotho, Ghana) and more than 8 (Cameroon, Côte d'Ivoire, Mauritania, Nigeria, Senegal); see Acsadi, Johnson-Acsadi, and Bulatao, op. cit. note 6, p. 164.

49. See M.J. Swartz, "Some Cultural Influences on Family Size in Three East African Societies," *Anthropological Quarterly,* vol. 42, no. 2 (1969), p. 73–88; see also A. Oyemade and T.A. Ogunmuyiwa, "Socio-Cultural Factors and Fertility in a Rural Nigerian Community," *Studies in Family Planning,* vol. 12, no. 3 (1981), p. 109ff.

50. Swartz, op. cit. note 49. This is also the case for other, non-African religions such as Hinduism.

51. See G.T.F. Acsadi and G. Johnson-Acsadi, "Demand for Children and Child Spacing," in Acsadi, Johnson-Acsadi, and Bulatao, op. cit. note 6, p. 155ff.

52. Frank and McNicoll offer an excellent description of the traditional factors that regulate fertility in African countries. See O. Frank and G. McNicoll, "An Interpretation of Fertility and Population Policy in Kenya," *Population and Development Review,* vol. 13, no. 2 (1987), pp. 209–43. See also P.B. Adongo, J.F. Phillips, and F.N. Binka, "The Influence of Traditional Religion on Fertility Regulation among the Kassena-Nankana of Northern Ghana," *Studies in Family Planning,* vol. 29, no. 1 (1998), p. 23ff.

53. See World Bank, *World Development Report 1984* (New York: Oxford University Press, 1984), p. 60.

54. It was Harvey Leibenstein who brought this aspect into the economic population theory; see *Economic Backwardness and Economic Growth* (New York: John Wiley, 1957). For the controversial debate on this aspect, see Farooq and Simmons, op. cit. note 4, p. 84ff. D. De Tray points out that important ethnic and regional differences exist in this regard, in "Children's Work Activities in Malaysia," *Population and Development Review,* vol. 9, no. 3 (1983), p. 437ff.

55. See S. Cochrane, V. Kozel, and H. Alderman, *Household Consequences of High Fertility in Pakistan,* World Bank Discussion Paper No. 111 (Washington, DC: World Bank, 1990), p. 27f., and the literature mentioned therein.

56. For an acute discussion of this complex matter, see R. Marcus and C. Harper, *Small Hands: Children in the Working World,* Save the Children Working Paper No. 16 (London: Save the Children,

1997). See also Save the Children (ed.), *Stitching Footballs* (London: 1997); C. Petty and M. Brown (eds.), *Justice for Children: Challenges for Policy and Practice in Sub-Saharan Africa* (London: Save the Children, 1998); International Labour Organisation, *Child Labor: Targeting the Intolerable* (Geneva: 1996); and UNICEF/Save the Children Sweden, *What Works for Working Children* (Smedjebacken: 1998).

57. See World Bank, op. cit. note 53, p. 59f.

58. E.M. King and R.E. Evenson, "Time Allocation and Home Production in Philippine Rural Households," in M. Buvinic, M. Lycette, and W. P. McGreevey, *Women and Poverty in the Third World* (Baltimore, MD: Johns Hopkins University Press, 1983), p. 35ff.; see also E.M. King, "The Effects of Family Size on Family Welfare: What Do We Know?" in D.G. Johnson and R.D. Lee (eds.), *Population Growth and Economic Development: Issues and Evidence* (Madison: University of Wisconsin Press, 1987), p. 373ff.

59. World Bank, op. cit. note 53, p. 59.

60. See, for example, M.T. Cain, "The Economic Activities of Children in a Village in Bangladesh," *Population and Development Review*, vol. 3, no. 3 (1977), p. 201; see also S. Anand and J. Morduch, *Poverty and the Population Problem: Evidence from Bangladesh* (Cambridge, MA: Harvard Institute for International Development, 1998).

61. IFPRI, *Food for Education* (Washington, DC: 2001).

62. A great variety of information and literature on human rights violations affecting children and the psychological and social consequences resulting from such violations is available, for example, through Amnesty International, UNICEF, and Save the Children.

Chapter 7, "Prerequisites for Responsible Population Policies"

1. C. Bright, "The Nemesis Effect," *World Watch*, June 1999, p. 12ff.

2. German Parliamentary Enquiry Commission, "Vorsorge zum Schutz der Erdatmosphäre": Schutz der Erde (ed.), *Mehr Zukunft für die Erde. Nachhaltige Energiepolitik für dauerhafte Klimaschutz* (Bonn: Economica Verlag, 1994), p. 41ff.; for further details on the topic of climate change, see Intergovernmental Panel on Climate Change (IPCC), *Climate Change 1994* (New York: Cambridge University Press, 1995).

3. World Resources Institute (WRI), United Nations Development Programme (UNDP), United Nations Environment Programme (UNEP), and World Bank, *World Resources 1998–99* (New York: Oxford University Press, 1998).

4. WRI, UNEP, and UNDP, *World Resources 1994–95* (New York: Oxford University Press, 1994), p. 200.

5. Population Reference Bureau, *1999 World Population Data Sheet* (Washington, DC: 1999).

6. WRI et al., op. cit. note 3, p. 344f.

7. Example of weighting calculation: The ratio of 10.2 tons of carbon dioxide emissions per capita in Germany to 1.0 tons in India, multiplied by the population of Germany in 1999 (82 million) = 836 million.

8. WRI et al., op. cit. note 3, p. 170.

9. In this regard, see the opinions expressed by M. King, "Health Is a Sustainable State," *The Lancet*, 15 September 1990, pp. 664–67, and by C. Ekkiot, "Legitimate Double-Think," *The Lancet*, 13 March 1993, pp. 669–72.

10. See D. Callahan, "Ethics and Population Limitation," in M.D. Bayles (ed.), *Ethics and Population* (Cambridge, MA: Schenkman, 1976), pp. 19–40.

11. Deutsche Gesellschaft für die Vereinten Nationen, *Aktionsprogramm der Konferenz der Vereinten Nationen über Bevölkerung und Entwicklung (ICPD)*. Published as *Blaue Reihe No. 54* (Bonn), December 1994, p. 11ff.

12. This would amount to "contraceptive imperialism," according to a pastoral letter issued by African bishops. See E. Schockenhoff, *Genug Platz für alle?* (Ostfildern, Germany: Schwabenverlag, 1992), p. 77; "Ethische Prinzipien der Bevölkerungspolitik und der Familienplanung," in H. Baumgartner, W. Bähm, and M. Lindauer (eds.), *Fortschritt als Schicksal? Weder Verheissung noch Verhängnis* (Stuttgart and Leipzig: Ernst Klett, 1996), pp. 83–100.

13. See, for example, the critical essay by I. Pinn and U. Nebelung, "Das Menschenbild in der Bevölkerungstheorie und Bevölkerungspolitik. Deutsche Traditionslinien vom 'klassischen' Rassismus bis zur Gegenwart," *Peripherie* (Germany), no. 37 (1989), pp. 21–50. See also R. Rott, "Bevölkerungskontrolle, Familienplanung und Geschlechterpolitik," *Peripherie*, no. 36 (1989), pp. 7–24.

14. Albert Schweitzer, *Christianity and the Religions of the World* (London: Allan and Unwin, 1939).

15. See United Nations Population Fund (UNFPA), *The State of World Population 1998: The New Generations* (New York: 1998).

16. See the discussion by J. Rawls, *A Theory of Justice* (Cambridge, MA: Belknap Press, 1999), chapters 1, 2, and 4. See also F. Böckle, H.R. Hemmer, and H. Kötter, *Armut und Bevölkerungsentwicklung in der Dritten Welt* (Bonn: Wissenschaftliche Arbeitsgruppe für weltkirchliche Aufgaben der Deutschen Bischofskonferenz, 1990), p. 20f.

17. See, for example, L.R. Brown, *Who Will Feed China?* (New York: Norton, 1995).

18. Jan Narveson, for example, believes that moral questions are predicated on the existence of human beings. Since this prerequisite is not fulfilled in the case of the unborn (or life not yet conceived), there is no moral reason to protect them from harm.

19. G. Hardin, "The Tragedy of the Commons," in M.D. Bayles (ed.), *Ethics and Population* (Cambridge, MA: Schenkman, 1976), pp. 3–18.

20. On this question, see A.F. Utz, "Sozialethik, III. Teil, Die soziale Ordnung," in A.F. Utz et al., (eds.), *Sammlung Politeia* (Bonn: IfG Verlagsgesellschaft mbH, 1986).

21. UNFPA, *The State of World Population 1997: The Right to Choose* (New York: 1997), p. 1. The Alan Guttmacher Institute (AGI) estimates there are approximately 80 million abortions annually. See AGI, *Sharing Responsibility: Women, Society, and Abortion Worldwide* (New York: 1999).

22. UNFPA, op. cit. note 21, p. 21.

23. O. Höffe (ed.), *Lexikon der Ethik*, 5th rev. ed. (Munich: C.H. Beck, 1997), p. 13.

24. For a comprehensive discussion of ethical questions in the context of human life, see E. Schockenhoff, *Ethik des Lebens. Ein theologischer Grundriß* (Mainz: Matthias Brünewald, 1993); see also L. Lassonde, *Coping with Population Challenges* (London: Earthscan, 1997).

25. See Chapter 7, "Reproductive Rights and Reproductive Health," at <http://www.iisd.ca/linkages/Cairo/program/p07000.html>.

Chapter 8, "The Battle for a Better Future"

1. S. Forman and R. Gosh, *The Reproductive Health Approach to Population and Development: Paying for the Essentials* (New York: New York University, Center on International Co-operation, 1999).

2. A. Grübler, "The Past and Future of Technology and the Environment," *IIASA* (International Institute for Applied Systems Analysis, Laxenburg, Austria) *Options*, winter 1998, p. 14.

3. E.U. von Weizsäcker, A.B. Lovins, and L.H. Lovins, *Faktor Vier. Doppelter Wohlstand—halbierter Naturverbrauch* (Munich: Droemer Knaur, 1995).

4. See Grübler, op. cit. note 2, p. 12ff.

5. FAO, *FAO Statement on Biotechnology,* <http://www.fao.org/biotech/stat.asp>.

6. See J.M. Staubl, "High-Yield Production of a Human Therapeutic Protein in Tobacco Chloroplasts," *Nature Biotechnology*, March 2000, pp. 333–38.

7. M. McGloughlin, "Ten Reasons Why Biotechnology Will Be Important to the Developing World," in University of Missouri (ed.), *The Economics of Biotechnology in Developing Countries*, at <www.agbioforum.org>; T. Arakawa, D.K.X. Chong, and W.H.R. Langridge, "Efficacy of a Plant-Based Oral Cholera Toxin B Subunit Vaccine," *Nature Biotechnology*, vol. 16 (1998), pp. 292–97; T. A. Haq, H.S. Mason, J.D. Clements, and C.J. Arntzen, "Oral Immunization with a Recombinant Bacterial Antigen Produced in Transgenic Plants," *Science*, no. 268 (1995), pp. 714–16; and C.O. Tacket, H.S. Mason, G. Losonsky, J.D. Clements, M.M. Levine, and C. Arntzen, "Immunogenicity of a Recombinant Bacterial Antigen Delivered in a Transgenic Potato," *Nature Medicine*, vol. 4, no. 5 (1998), pp. 607–09.

8. See I. Potrykus (ed.), *New Horizons in Swiss Plant Biotechnology: From the Laboratory to the Field*, proceedings of a symposium organized at the ETH Zurich on the occasion of the 125th anniversary of the Department of Agronomy and Food Sciences, Zurich, 1996; see also A.F. Krattiger and A. Rosemarin (eds.), *Biosafety for Sustainable Agriculture* (Stockholm: Stockholm Environment Institute, 1994), section 1.

9. H.W. Kendall, R. Beachy, T. Eisner, F. Gould, R. Herdt, P.H. Raven, J.S. Schell, and M.S. Swaminathan, *Bioengineering of Crops: Report of the World Bank Panel on Transgenic Crops*, Environmentally and Socially Sustainable Development Studies and Monographs Series 23 (Washington, DC: World Bank, 1997), p. 15.

10. ISI/Fraunhofer Institut für Systemtechnik und Innovationsforschung, Delphi 1998 Umfrage, *Studie zur Globalen Entwicklung von Wissenschaft und Technik (im Auftrag des Bundesministeriums für Bildung und Forschung)* (Karlruhe, Germany: 1998).

11. Royal Society of London, *Transgenic Plants and World Agriculture* (London: 2000). Similar arguments are put forward by the Indian Council of Agricultural Research; see M. Rai and B. M. Prasanna, *Transgenics in Agriculture* (New Delhi: Indian Council of Agricultural Research, 2000).

12. See M.H. Daniell, *World of Risks: Next Generation Strategy for a Volatile Era* (Singapore: John Wiley, 2000), p. 11.

13. K.M. Leisinger, "Disentangling Risk Issues," in G.J. Persley (ed.), *Biotechnology for Developing Country Agriculture: Problems and Opportunities*, 2020 Focus 2, (Washington, DC: International Food Policy Research Institute [IFPRI], 1999), p. 1.

14. National Research Council, *Field Testing Genetically Modified Organisms: Framework for Decision* (Washington, DC: National Academy Press, 1989).

15. J.J. Cohen (ed.), *Managing Agricultural Biotechnology: Addressing Research Program Needs and Policy Implications* (London: CAB International, 1999); see also the excellent overview study organized and financed by the German foundation Friedrich-Ebert-Stiftung: M. Quain and D. Virchow, *Macht die Grüne Gentechnik die Welt satt? Herausforderungen für Forschung, Politik und Gesellschaft* (Bonn: Friedrich-Ebert-Stiftung, 1999).

16. See <www.agbioworld.org>, viewed 8 March 2000.

17. See M.K. Sears, D.E. Stanlex-Horn, and H.R. Mattila, *Preliminary Report on the Ecological Impact of Bt Corn Pollen on the Monarch Butterfly in Ontario* (Guelph, ON, Canada: University of Guelph, 17 January 2000); see also Mark K. Sears, "Comments on Recent Reports Dealing with Bt Corn and the Monarch Butterfly," *Crop Pest Ontario*, 25 August 2000.

18. S.B. Lehrer, "The Potential Health Risks of Genetically Modified Organisms: How Can Allergens Be Assessed and Minimized?" at the International Conference on Ensuring Food Security, Protecting the Environment, Reducing Poverty in Developing Countries: Can Biotechnology Help? Washington, DC, 21–22 October 1999.

19. See also M. Quaim, A.F. Krattiger, and J. von Braun, *Agricultural Biotechnology in Developing Countries: Towards Optimizing the Benefits for the Poor* (Boston: Kluwer, 2000), pp. 11–23.

20. National Academy of Sciences, *Introduction of Recombinant DNA-Engineered Organisms into the Environment: Key Issues* (Washington, DC: National Academy Press, 1987).

21. Ed Susman, "Gene-Altered Food Appears Safe," *UPI Science News*, 3 December 2000.

22. See the closing address of the 6th International Symposium on the Biosafety of Genetically Modified Organisms by Alan McHughen <www.usask.ca/agriculture/biosafety/committee.html>.

23. For discussion of the successes, see R. Barker, R.W. Herdt, and B. Rose, *The Rice Economy of Asia* (Washington, DC: Resources for the Future, 1985); for discussion of the failures, see A. Pearce, *Seeds of Plenty, Seeds of Want* (Oxford: Clarendon Press, 1980).

24. During the preparation of this book, the International Rice Research Institute announced the introduction of a new high-yielding rice variety that could raise global output by 10–15 percent; see Dolly Aglay, Reuters, 14 March 2000.

25. See the 50 particularly impressive examples in the new report to the Club of Rome by E.U. von Weizsäcker, A.B. Lovins, and L.H. Lovins, *Faktor Vier. Doppelter Wohlstand – halbierter Naturverbrauch* (Munich: Droemer Knaur, 1995).

26. In this context, it is worth remembering the last *Spiegel* interview with Hans Jonas, in which he expressed doubt whether democracy based on plebiscite and the short-term preservation of interests was the most suitable form of government to avoid an environmental crisis or achieve an ecological turnaround; see *Der Spiegel*, 11 May 1992, p. 92ff. Jonas did, however, admit that he could not think of a better alternative to present-day democracy.

27. In emission certificates, the state defines the highest permissible overall emissions and issues permits that grant the right to emit a specific volume of harmful substances. These certificates are traded—that is, companies can buy them and may resell them if they are unable or unwilling to use them. Companies that try to reduce emissions of harmful substances can cut costs by avoiding the need to purchase such certificates. Carbon or environmental taxes are levied when the main objective is to change behavior patterns. A tax is therefore charged in order to reduce environmental stress. Although no binding rules on terminology exist, direct or environmental taxes are often referred to when the earnings due to the taxpayers are repaid in another form. If the earnings are not reimbursed and the tax is primarily aimed at covering the insatiable needs of the state for funds, it is referred to as an "ecotax."

28. See A. Gärres, H. Ehringhaus, and E.U. von Weizsäcker, *Der Weg zur ökologischen Steuerreform. Weniger Umweltbelastung und mehr Beschäftigung* (Munich: Olzog Verlag, 1994).

29. See F. Schmidt-Bleek, *Wieviel Umwelt braucht der Mensch? Das Mass für ökologisches Wirtschaften* (Basel: Birkhäuser, 1994).

30. German Advisory Council on Global Change, *Welt im Wandel.: Wege zur Lösung globaler Umweltprobleme*, 1995 Annual Report (Berlin: 1996).

31. Wuppertal Institute for Climate, Environment, and Energy, *Zukunftsfägiges Deutschland. Ein Beitrag zu einer global nachhaltigen Entwicklung* (Basel: Birkhäuser, 1996), p. 166.

32. "Affluence lite" from ibid.

33. For this argument, see V. Hösle, *Philosophie der ökologischen Krise*, Beck'sche Reihe (Munich: C.H. Beck, 1991), p. 88ff. Of course, this way of thinking is also applicable to the population prob-

lem in developing countries. Where is the motivation for an individual couple in sub-Saharan Africa to do without the additional social security of a fourth, fifth, or sixth child? In states whose deficiencies in good governance often present a direct threat to individual welfare, it makes sense that individuals would want to rely on the traditional security system of the extended family.

34. S. Dunn, "Coal Use Continues Rebound," in L.R. Brown et al., *Vital Signs 1998* (New York: Norton, 1998), p. 52.

35. "Global Public Opinion on the Environment 1998," *The Environmental Monitor,* International Report, Washington, DC, 1999.

36. Deutsche Stiftung Weltbevölkerung and United Nations Population Fund (eds.), *Bevölkerung und nachhaltige Entwicklung—Fünf Jahre nach Rio* (Hannover: 1998); see also <www.dsw-online.de>.

Index

Abortion: arguments in favor of, 108–109; of female fetus, 94; opponents of, 109

Absolute poverty. *See* Poverty

Acid rain, 10

Affluence lite model, 125

Africa: famine-related issues in, 62, 67–68; food-insecure people in, 64–66, 73; food production in, 69–70; social deprivation in, 8–9; spread of HIV/AIDS in, 15

Aging population, 13–14

Agricultural growth: biotechnology's role in, 116–118; improving food availability with, 74; public investments for increasing, 75–76

Agricultural land, soil degradation of, 50–51

Agricultural sector: aging population impact on, 14; water consumption in, 43–45

AIDS. *See* HIV/AIDS

American Medical Association (AMA), 120

Arable land: in developing countries, 49; irrigated farming and, 43–44

Asia: biodiversity loss in, 56; child labor issues in, 93–95; food-insecure people in, 64–65, 73; food production in, 70; population growth rate in, 3–4; pressure on food supplies in, 33–34

Bailey, Ronald, 16

Bengal famine, 60

Berlin Conference on Climate, 124

Biodiversity: loss of, 55–56; protection of, 127, 128

Biotechnology: benefit/risk assessment of, 118–120; contribution to food security, 116–118; in developing countries, 120–121; public acceptance of, 121

Birdsall, Nancy, 34

Birth rates, 2; in developing countries, 25, 79–80; education's role in lowering, 81–82, 85–86, 107; food supplies and, 33–34; impact on labor market, 36–37; impact on permanent investments, 36; mortality rates and, 26–27; social costs of high, 31–34; sociocultural norms' influence on, 77

Brown, Lester, 16, 28

Caldwell, J. C., 79

Caloric inadequacy. *See* Food insecurity

Capital formation, reduction in, 35–36

Carter, Jimmy, 53

Cereal production: criteria for judging, 68–69; demand for, 70–71, 73. *See also* Food production

Cereal yields, 66, 72

Child(ren): as caretaker of elderly, 88–89; as an economic factor, 89–92; exploitation of, 91; human rights and, 91–95; labor, 90–91; malnutrition, 83; marriages, 94; position in traditional societies, 86–87; production activities of, 90

Child mortality rate: in developing countries, 5, 8, 33, 94; women's education in lowering, 82–83

China: cereal and meat demand in, 70–71; famine-related deaths in, 61; food-inse-

cure people in, 64; fossil fuel use in, 126; irrigation technology improvements in, 46–47; population forecasting of, 20; population growth rate in, 3–4; present vs. future generations well-being in, 105–106; urbanization trends in, 12
Chronic food insecurity, 58
CO$_2$ emissions: environmental costs and, 123; restricting global, 98
Coale, Ansley, 25
Cognitive development, 63
Contagious diseases, progress in controlling, 5
Crop-breeding programs, 117
Crude birth rates. *See* Birth rates
Cultural norms, 77

Deforestation: as ecological threat, 10; soil erosion and, 50
Demeny, Paul, 25
Demographic fatigue, 28
Demographic transition: demographic trap and, 27–28; European pattern of, 25, 27
Demographic trends: aging population, 13–14; forecast of, 20; spread of HIV/AIDS, 15; urbanization, 11–13
Desertification, food security problems with, 51
Developing countries: aging population in, 13; arable land availability in, 49; biotechnology's role in, 120–121; birth rates in, 25, 79–80; cereal and meat demand in, 70–71, 73; children's position in, 88–92; development policy in, 100; drinking water problems in, 42; ecological progress in, 6–7; ecological threats in, 9–10; economic deprivation in, 9; economic progress in, 6; education for women in, 81–82; energy consumption in, 98–99; environmental issues in, 126; food-insecure people in, 64–65; food security in, 6, 8–9, 75–76; human rights issues in, 92–95; income inequality in, 38; investment structure changes in, 36; irrigated area in, 44; labor market problems in, 36–37; life expectancy in, 4, 8; migration problems of, 38–39; mortality rates in, 5, 8, 25–26, 32, 33; population policy for,

24; pressure on food supplies in, 33–34; reduction in capital formation in, 35; social deprivation in, 8–9; social progress in, 4–5; soil erosion in, 48–49; traditional societies in, 78–80; transfer of technology in, 122–123; water shortages in, 41–42; ways to increase agricultural growth in, 75; women's political and economic rights in, 83–86
Development policy, population policies and, 99–100
Diet deficiency. *See* Food insecurity
Discrimination: against girls, 33; against women, 79, 86
Domestic violence, 94
Dowry system, 33, 94
Drinking water problems, 42
Drip irrigation, water savings with, 47

Ecological progress: in developing countries, 6–7; labor market problems and, 37
Ecological tax reform, 123
Ecological threats: population growth and, 9–10; resource efficiency revolution and, 122, 124, 127
Economic deprivation, 9
Economic disadvantages: capital formation reduction, 35–36; changes in the investment structure, 36; income inequality, 38; labor market problems, 36–37; migration, 38–39
Economic progress: in developing countries, 6; population factor and, 22
Economic rights for women, 80–81
Education: birth rate impact on, 34; role in lowering birth rates, 81–82, 85–86, 107; women's right to, 81–83, 94
Ehrlich, Anne, 16
Elderly, children as caretaker of, 88–89
Employment: birth rate impact on, 36–37; irrigated farming for increasing, 44–45
Energy consumption: as ecological threat, 9; in industrial and developing countries, 98–99; population problem and, 16–17
Environmental problems. *See* Global environmental problems

Environmental space concept, 97–99

Erosion. *See* Soil erosion

Ethical dilemmas: abortion, 108–109; individual well-being vs. public welfare, 106–108; present vs. future generations well-being, 105–106

Ethiopian famine, 60, 61

Europe: demographic transition in, 25, 27; famine-related deaths in, 61; mortality rates in, 25–26

Evenson, R. E., 89

Extended families, 78–79

Families: birth rate impact on, 31–34, 37; food-insecure, 63, 66. *See also* Traditional societies

Family income, children's contribution to, 89–92

Family planning: men and, 80–86; religious norms and, 87; in traditional societies, 78

Famine: in Africa, 62, 67–68; causes of, 61–62; poverty and, 60

Farmers: cereal production demand and, 72; economic incentives for, 52

Fertility rate, 1, 13–14

Food and Agriculture Organization (FAO), 44, 58, 117

Food availability: agricultural growth for improving, 74–75; food production and, 59–60

Food for Schooling program, 92

Food-insecure people: distribution of, 64; features of, 66; number of, 73; as share of total population, 65

Food insecurity: causes of, 59–62; consequences of, 62–63; defined, 58; food production decline and, 67–70; poverty and, 60; types of, 58–59

Food production: arable land availability for, 49; food availability and, 59–60; with irrigated farming, 45; population growth and, 69; projections of, 73–74, 76; rise in, 67; soil erosion issues and, 49–50; technology's role in, 69–70; women's role in, 68, 84–85

Food security: biotechnology contribution to,

116–118, 121; defined, 58; desertification and, 51; in developing countries, 6, 8–9; introduction to, 57; policies for, 74–76; prospects for assuring, 70–74; urbanization trends and, 12; women's role in providing, 68, 84–85

Food supplies, birth rate impact on, 33–34

Food unavailability, 59–60

Foreign capital, 35

Forest degradation: factors influencing, 54; population growth and, 53–55

Fourth World Conference on Women, 109

Fresh water. *See* Water consumption

Galbraith, John Kenneth, 68

Gender relations, 79–80

Genetic engineering: benefit/risk assessment of, 118–120; contribution to food security, 116–118; in developing countries, 120–121; public acceptance of, 121

Genetic modification (GM) technology, 118

Girls: as child labor, 92; discrimination against, 33, 93–94; right to education, 94

Global demilitarization, 7

Global environmental problems: environmentally friendly lifestyle and, 124–126; environmental space concept and, 97–98; individual contributions to solving, 126; technology's role in solving, 127–128. *See also* Ecological threats

Greenhouse effect, 98, 114

Green Revolution, 120

Hardin, Garrett, 107

Haub, Carl, 21

HIV/AIDS: increase in spread of, 15; involving men in discussions about, 81

Human rights: children and, 91–94; human dignity and, 95; individual well-being vs. public welfare and, 107; reproductive decisions and, 103–104; violations, 93–94

Human values, population growth and, 100–101

Hunger. *See* Food insecurity

Income gap/inequality: birth rate impact on,

38; in developing vs. industrial countries, 9

India: agricultural needs in, 14; child labor issues in, 95; food-insecure people in, 64; fossil fuel use in, 126; irrigation technology improvements in, 46–47; population growth rate in, 3–4; urbanization trends in, 12

Indonesia, population growth rate in, 3–4

Industrial countries: cereal and meat demand in, 71; energy consumption in, 98–99; environmental issues in, 126; food-insecure people in, 64; food production rise in, 67; innovation required in, 122–123; irrigated area in, 44; life expectancy in, 8; water consumption in, 42–43; women's political and economic rights in, 83–86

Industrialization as demographic trend, 27

Infant mortality: in developing countries, 33; women's education in lowering, 82–83

Infectious diseases, poor diet and, 59

Infertility: family planning and, 87; traditional societies and, 78–79

Innovation: in industrial countries, 122–123; promotion of, 122–123

International Conference on Population and Development, 4, 101, 110

International Labour Organisation (ILO), 36

International Model for Policy Analysis of Commodities and Trade (IMPACT), 70

Investment structure, birth rate impact on, 36

Irish famine, 60, 61

Irrigated farming: increasing employment opportunities with, 44–45; social costs related to, 45; water consumption and, 42–44

Irrigation technology, 46–47

Jonas, Hans, 21

Keyfitz, Nathan, 20

King, E. M., 89

Labor market, birth rate impact on, 36–37

Latin America, food-insecure people in, 64–66

Law of the Minimum, 24

Levi-Strauss company, 92

Life expectancy, 4, 8

Livestock. *See* Meat production

Malnutrition. *See* Food insecurity

Malthus, Thomas Robert, 16, 23, 24, 69, 70

Maternal health, education's role in promoting, 83

Maternal mortality, 32

McNamara, Robert, 60

Meat production, demand for, 70–71

Men: family planning and, 80–86; responsibility for reproductive behavior, 110–111; status and role of, 78–80

Messerli, B., 51

Migration: food security issues and, 63; how to solve, 39; reason for trends in, 38–39

Military spending, political developments and, 7

Modernization process: alternative ideals of, 124–127; child work significance and, 90; women's changing role and, 89

Moral dilemmas: abortion, 108–109; individual well-being vs. public welfare, 106–108; present vs. future generations well-being, 105–106

Morbidity, food insecurity and, 62

Mortality rates: birth rates and, 26–27; of children, 5, 8, 33, 82–83, 94; maternal, 32; population growth and, 25–26

Museveni, President Yoweri, 68

Natural systems: biodiversity loss, 55–56; forest degradation, 53–55; fresh water, 41–48; soil erosion, 48–52

Nigeria, population growth rate in, 3–4

Nutritional needs/status: of boys and girls, 33–34; of healthy adults, 58; in India, 14; spread of HIV/AIDS and, 15

Organisation for Economic Co-Operation and Development, 9

Overpopulation, concept of, 22

Ozone layer, 127

Pakistan, population growth rate in, 3–4

Political developments, role of state in new, 7
Political rights, 80–81
Political shortcomings, sustainable development and, 10
Population factor, importance of, 21–23
Population forecasting: criteria in, 21; value of, 21; weakness in making, 20–21
Population growth: by billions, 2; biodiversity loss and, 55–56; current and projected, 2–4; ecological threats and, 9–10; economic deprivation and, 9; economic disadvantages of, 34–39; factors influencing future, 19–20; human values and, 100–101; impact on forest degradation, 53–55; impact on soil erosion, 48–52; impact on water consumption, 41–48; social deprivation and, 8–9; social impact of, 31–34; too little or too much, 21–23; understanding patterns of, 23–29; urbanization trends in, 11–13; water shortage problems and, 41–42. See also Food production; Global environmental problems
Population policies: aims of, 100–102; for developing countries, 24; development policy and, 99–100; discussions about, 28–29; environmental space concept and, 97–99; ethically acceptable, 102–103; ethically legitimate, 103–105; moral dilemmas related to, 105–109; reproductive behavior and, 101, 109–110; water consumption issues and, 45–46
Population problem: optimistic views about, 17–18; pessimistic views about, 15–17; Population Reference Bureau, 21
Poverty: absolute, 60; child labor and, 90–91; food insecurity and, 60; in sub-Saharan Africa, 37; urbanization trends and, 12
Pregnancy: abortion and, 108; maternal deaths and, 32

Quisumbing, Agnes, 85

Rain forests, 53, 55
Religious norms, 77, 86–87
Repression and violence. See Violence
Reproductive behavior, 101, 109–110

Reproductive decisions: freedom of making, 106, 107; human rights and, 103–105
Reproductive health, 33; abortion and, 108–109; family planning and, 80–81
Resource efficiency revolution, 122, 124, 127
Rosegrant, Mark, 42, 47
Rural areas, food insecurity in, 58

Sadik, Nafis, 31
Scherr, Sara, 49, 51
Schweitzer, Albert, 102
Sen, Amartya, 60
Simon, Julian, 16, 17, 28
Social deprivation, 8–9
Social norms, 77
Social progress in developing countries, 4–5
Soil erosion/degradation: of agricultural land, 50–51; in developing countries, 48–49; food production and, 49–50; forest degradation and, 54–55; ways to combat, 51–52; with weather changes, 51
Somalia, famine-related deaths in, 61
South Asia. See Asia
Starvation. See Food insecurity
Sub-Saharan Africa, 1, 33; food insecurity issues in, 64–65, 68, 73; food production in, 67, 69, 70; poverty rate in, 37
Sufficiency revolution, 124
Süssmilch, Johann Peter, 15
Sustainable development, 99; environmental costs and, 123–124; innovation as road to, 122–123; integral policies for, 113–114; modernization ideals and, 126; pessimistic and optimistic views about, 114–116; political shortcomings and, 10; promotion of, 7, 100, 109

Taliban rulers of Afghanistan, 94
Tax shifting, 123
Technology: innovation for transfer of, 122–123; limits of, 127; role in food production, 69–70; sustainable development and, 114–116, 126
Teklu, Tesfaye, 62
Tertullianus, Quintus Septimus, 1
Third World Academy of Sciences, 118

Traditional societies: children and human rights in, 92–95; children as caretakers in, 88–92; children's position in, 86–87; family planning issues in, 80–81; role of men and women in, 78–79; women's education in, 82

Transgenic crops, 120

Transitory food insecurity, 58

Tropical forests, 54, 55, 56

U.S. National Academy of Sciences, 120

U.S. National Research Council, 119

United Nations Conference on Environment and Development, 9

United Nations Development Programme, 7

United Nations Population Fund, 31, 34, 54, 79, 84, 108

Universal Declaration of Human Rights, 101, 103, 104

Urban areas, food insecurity in, 58

Urbanization, 11–13, 27, 89

Violence: dowry system and, 94; as political shortcoming, 10

von Braun, Joachim, 62

Water-and wind-induced erosion, 49

Water consumption: demand for, 42; in developing and industrial countries, 41–43; distribution conflicts related to, 45–46; as ecological threat, 10; irrigated farming and, 42–45; for private and industrial use, 41

Water savings: drip irrigation as method for, 47; ways to increase, 46

Water shortages: in developing countries, 41–42; policy recommendations for handling, 47–48

Weather changes, soil degradation and, 51

Webb, Patrick, 62

Women: abortion and, 109; modernization process and, 89; political and economic rights for, 83–84; poverty and, 60; right to education, 81–83; role in food production, 68, 84–85; status and role of, 78–80

World Health Organization (WHO), 15, 42

World population: age 60 and older, 13–14; by billions, 2, 5; current and projected, 2–4, 127; growth rate in, 3; spread of HIV/AIDS in, 15; urban and rural shares of, 11

World Resources Institute, 98

About the Authors

Klaus M. Leisinger is the executive director and delegate of the Board of Trustees of the Novartis Foundation for Sustainable Development, and the executive director ad interim of the Syngenta Foundation for Sustainable Agriculture.

Karin M. Schmitt is the director for social development programs of the Novartis Foundation for Sustainable Development in Basel, Switzerland. She is in charge of issues related to social development and human rights, and she also manages the foundation's external communications.

Rajul Pandya-Lorch is head of the 2020 Vision for Food, Agriculture, and the Environment initiative of the International Food Policy Research Institute in Washington, D.C. She writes and speaks extensively on global food security issues.